Red Arrow Men

MAJOR GENERAL WILLIAM H. GILL
Commander, 32nd (Red Arrow Division)

Red Arrow Men

Stories About the 32nd Division on the Villa Verde

By John M. Carlisle

Drawings by Joe Ash

Arnold-Powers, Inc.
Detroit

Copyright 1945 • JOHN M. CARLISLE

Printed in the United States of America

DEDICATION

THE AMERICAN SOLDIER *at war is a tremendous fellow with an unusual capacity for courage and ingenuity, stamina and just plain guts. Nowhere in the history of World War II was the American soldier called upon to show more daring and head-on bravery than GI Joe of the Thirty-Second Division during the Villa Verde operation.*

For 119 days the fighting Red Arrow Division fought up the winding hairpin turns of the Villa Verde Trail. High in the Caraballo Mountains of Northern Luzon, against a determined, fanatical enemy who elected to fight and die where he was dug in.

This was a mauling fight against the Jap in his remarkable defensive positions, against the terrain, supply and climate. In those 119 days the Red Arrow boys fought 22 miles, sometimes 35 yards at a time, with the Jap never more than 30 feet away. The division killed 9,000 Japs and took 50 prisoners. It lost 4,226 men, about a third of the division strength.

In this operation, as a civilian, was amazed what GI Joe, just the ordinary guy in his foxhole, could do and did.

They outbid the imagination in this daily routine, and through it all he dreamed and thought of home.

While I was living with these Red Arrow veterans of the

Villa Verde, it occurred to me again and again that while true democracy was fighting to preserve its way of life, GI Joe was fighting to get home.

The Red Arrow veteran epitomized the spirit of the American Army, one of the most magnificent in the history of war, a determination to fight like hell and then get home. For our soldiers in the Southwest Pacific saw a lot of the world, and the more they saw the more they liked the home they had left with a reverence and a longing that sometimes seemed pitiful as they sat under ponchon in little foxholes half filled with water on Caraballo Mountains.

And so, to these veterans of the Red Arrow Division, this book is respectfully dedicated in the hope that it somewhat preserves their flaming courage, daring and will to win on the Villa Verde Trail.

JOHN M. CARLISLE

FOREWORD

I CAN THINK OF no better tribute to the men of the 32d Division than this collection by Jack Carlisle. Jack was there. He saw the battle of the Villa Verde Trail unfold before his eyes. His story is a first-hand account of fighting over some of the most rugged terrain encountered in the entire Pacific War.

We of the 32d came to know Carlisle well in those days of the Villa Verde. He was with us during the most critical phase of the operation. On several occasions he accompanied me to the front. I saw him talk with many a front line infantryman. In the case of many Michigan men he brought them the first personal word they had from home in many long months of overseas service.

But Jack didn't talk only with the heroes. No man's story was too insignificant. He talked to all of the men, regardless of whether they were buck privates doing KP in a rear echelon or machine gunners on a mountain perimeter. They all got their names in the paper. They're all heroes, and he made them all heroes.

Throughout the Villa Verde operation, Carlisle showed a tireless determination to dig-out and record every phase of the Division's combat function. He recorded this story not in general terms but in specific terms of the individual GI in every echelon.

Carlisle tells more vividly than anyone to date the story of the Villa Verde.

The 32d went into action in the Sixth Army's I Corps Sector in Northern Luzon on January 30, 1945. Our mission was to drive 24 miles up into the Caraballo Mountains along the Villa Verde Trail to its junction with Highway 5 and thus secure one of the only two Southern approaches to the Cagayan Valley. The 25th Division was to drive up Highway 5 and meet us at Santa Fe, thus creating a pincer movement.

So, while other elements of the Sixth Army drove south toward Manila, the 32d and the 25th launched their pincer movement designed to open the way to the Cagayan Valley—which runs north to Aparri.

We found ourselves facing defenses prepared by an old enemy, Lieut. Gen. Tomoyuki Yamashita, the man they called "Tiger of Malaya" and "The Butcher of Bataan." The 32d had had a taste of his caves and pillboxes, his artillery and his concealed machine guns in the Ormoc Corridor on Leyte. We knew we were in for a tough assignment on the Villa Verde Trail from the very beginning.

Yamashita had done a more thorough job of his Villa Verde defenses than those on Leyte because he'd had more time.

It took us 119 days to secure the Villa Verde and during that time we killed 8900 Japs.

I hold the Villa Verde operation up as an example of what teamwork can do. Every element of this Division did a magnificent job. Without the work of the Engineers, the Medical Corps, the Artillery, the Quartermaster, Ordnance and all the supporting elements of the Division, our three infantry regiments, the 126th, 127th and 128th couldn't have done their job.

I shall always remember the 916 men who died in the winning of the Villa Verde. The pages of this book are a tribute to them.

We have here a segment of the Pacific War and the Pacific Victory. This is how it was done all the way from New Guinea up the "road back." It's typical of the blood, the struggle and the sacrifice.

On Sept. 2, 1945, Gen. Yamashita, the old Tiger himself came into the 32d's lines to surrender. It was a great moment for the 32d, a glorious finish to this long bitter struggle.

MAJ. GEN. W. H. GILL

TABLE OF CONTENTS

Chapter		Page
1	Death Stalks the Trail	13
2	Mines on Bamboo Poles	16
3	The Battle for Dog Hill	18
4	Daredevil Pilot Posts Yanks	21
5	Generals In Fox Holes	24
6	Yank "Valentines" For Japs	27
7	Sneak Attack on Hospital	30
8	32nd's Hours of Combat	34
9	The Laughing General	38
10	Lucky Oddities	42
11	Time Out For a Slugfest	46
12	A Laugh On the Japs	49
13	Forward on Hands and Knees	51
14	I Take a Tumble	55
15	The Sergeant Gets the Beer	57
16	A Senseless Banzai Charge	60
17	Planting TNT In A Cave of Japs	63
18	Seven WACS and Seven Joes	66
19	WACS on the Villa Verde Front	69
20	Nothing Stops the GI Road Gangs	73
21	"Brooklyn" Wins a Stripe	76
22	Engineers Work Miracles	78
23	In and Out of a Jap Ambush	82
24	Medics Are Heroic Too	85
25	A Note to Those Who Wait	88
26	Medics Never Rest	90
27	Red Blood Saves Lives	93
28	School Children Buy Mercy Planes	96
29	Messman Makes Mess For Japs	99
30	Time Out to Jest	102
31	Communiques Are Understatement	105
32	Builders and Fighters Both	108
33	Manila Bares A Wounded Heart	111

Chapter		Page
34	"The Little Man of Football"	115
35	119 Grueling Days	118
36	Not One Remained Alive	122
37	"Little Boy" Leads the Way	125
38	How They Got Their Stars for Gallantry	129
39	Villa Verde Is a Panorama of War	132
40	A Dress for a Filipino Girl	136
41	90 Pounds of Misery	138
42	The Colonel Was a School Teacher	141
43	The General Waits for the Private	144
44	Your Boy Died a Hero	147
45	El Lobo Means the Wolf	151
46	A Gallant Captain Lives in Memory	153
47	The Price of Successful War	156
48	Gill's Boys Get the Best	158
49	Memo of a Red Cross Girl	160
50	Red Cross Sparks Morale	162
51	Nurses Often Write For Them	164
52	A Place to Feel at Home	166
53	Jungle Juice for GI's	168
54	A Narrow Escape	170
55	Ambulance With Wings	172
56	Cause for Hatred	175
57	Smiling Through Cakes of Mud	177
58	To Marcos, the Igorot	180
59	78 Heroes Receive Medals	182
60	With a Catch in His Voice	185
61	Michigan Heroes Rate High	187
62	Jap Atrocities Invade a Dream	190
63	A Memory of Luzon	192
64	A Villa Verde Jeep	194
65	Vivid Memories For Home	198
66	Battle Casualties Are Always Game	200
67	Suicide Planes Attack Medics Too	203
68	Medics Scorn Snipers	205
69	Doctors and Cooks Combine to Save Lives	207
70	It's Painful to Say Goodbye	210
71	Yamashita	213

« 1 »

Death Stalks the Trail

THERE IS NO harder fighting by American troops anywhere on the far-flung war fronts of the world than on the Villa Verde Trail, 6,000 feet up in the Caraballo Mountains.

For 90 days, as this is written, the rugged troops of the 32nd Division have fought their way 20 miles up the foot-path trail, building a road with armored bulldozers, climbing up the precipitous ridges and hills on the flanks, fighting the Japs yard by yard.

In those 90 days the 32nd has killed 6,000 Japs, taken 24 prisoners and out-fought, out-gamed and out-maneuvered the best troops in the Japanese army.

This is a fight to the death up here in the clouds. The Japs won't retreat. They won't surrender. They dig in to die for their emperor.

They are dug in on the high ground in deep, well-camouflaged caves. They "look down the throats" of our boys and cover our positions with machine gun and mortar fire.

Our troops have to fight in the draws in the dense undergrowth, then up the slope. I watched two companies fight their way up a steep ridge for 35 yards in one day. Later that night they repulsed a sharp counterattack.

When our long-range machine guns, mortars and artillery open up, the Japs hide in their deep caves, dug into the slope of the ridge.

The Red Arrow troops of Maj.-Gen. William H. Gill fight their way against heavy machine gun fire up to these caves and seal them with demolition charges. Our troops dig trenches toward the caves, pushing sandbags ahead of them as they dig, until they get close enough to throw their demolition charges.

The sun is broiling hot. The fighting is at a close-up range of 30 feet.

The Jap resistance is stubborn and fanatical, but these are seasoned Yank troops, most of them with 37 months overseas, veterans of the steaming jungles of Buna, the kunai grass and flooded rivers of Saidor, the matted forests of Aitape and the muddy mountains of Leyte.

The Villa Verde Trail was cut through more than a half-century ago by a Spanish priest, Juan Villa Verde. It was a foot-path to bring religion to the Filipinos in the valley on the other side of the mountain.

This campaign over the trail has strategic military value of great importance to the campaign in Northern Luzon, and because of that its Jap defenders have been ordered to fight to the last man.

So, for the 32nd, it is a campaign of annihilation. But a division cannot move along a foot-path. It must have a road.

It is one of the great stories of the war how its engineers have built a road 8 to 12 feet wide, cutting away the sides of mountains and putting up bamboo rails as protection against deep cliffs, all under fire.

Right behind the infantrymen is an armored bulldozer, making the trail. The Jap snipers try to pick them off. Jap machine guns up the trail blaze away. The veteran "cat" (bulldozer) drivers have won the respect of the hard-bitten infantryman.

Our supplies and ammunition come up part of the way by truck, and then are relayed by Filipino carrier trains. A portable hospital has been built in a gully, and ambulances rumble down to it throughout every day.

The riflemen carry the brunt of the fight. Our valiant scouts and patrols feel out the enemy. Then the rifle companies go in. They crawl slowly down a slope, then slowly up an enemy-held slope—crawling, shooting, fighting. Scrub pine and coarse cogon grass cover the mountainside. Many of the slopes, though, are sparsely wooded, baking hot by day and freezing cold by night.

At night the Japs make Banzai attacks. They organize small suicidal squads, equipped with 10-pound and 20-pound "satchels" of TNT and dynamite set off by grenades. They creep up, wearing rubber "sneakers," and throw their murderous "satchels" into our defense.

The Yanks have perimeter defenses against these attacks. They always wipe out the Japs. Two riflemen in a foxhole take turns on the alert through the cold, freezing nights.

There never is a moment when the Yanks are safe anywhere on the road. Some of them have been knocked out by Jap artillery fire. Some of them have had land mines ahead of them. But the work goes on, every hour, every day. Almost inconceivable is the determination of the engineers.

This is, in fact, a "Little Burma Road," challenging all the pathways through the mountains to our positions, and going up to the front there is a four-mile stretch where the Japs on Yamashita Ridge, 1,200 yards away, and the Japs on Mt. Imugan, 2,000 yards away, sweep the trail with machine gun fire and 47 millimeter field pieces.

Every day and every night the fight goes on. The 32nd is winning it, against all odds, against all hardships. It is a great division and this campaign on the Villa Verde Trail will long be remembered in the military history of the American Army.

« 2 »

Mines on Bamboo Poles

OUR JEEP PARTY started up the Villa Verde Trail, after fording a small stream, at 6 a.m., long before breakfast, to take advantage of the cool early mornings of Luzon.

An MP checked traffic up ahead on the telephone and motioned us to start up the trail. The road, which the engineers had built under terrific handicaps, was small and we crawled around a sharp S turn in second.

Thick yellow silt lay heavy on the road, and our wheels churned up a heavy cloud of dust that could be seen for miles around. Our trip was just a succession of sharp S turns on the mountain road. All about us were ridges, high peaked mountains, and deep cliffs and gorges.

More than halfway up the 20-mile road, which was won by 90 days of hard fighting and is still uncompleted, while the fighting goes on, we stopped at one of our camps on the hillside.

I had breakfast with Chief Warrant Officer Morris Samsky, 2005 Philadelphia avenue west, Detroit; a very good breakfast of cream of wheat, one egg, wheat cakes and syrup, and hot coffee.

Samsky and Sergt. Fred A. Pomeroy, 8990 Helen avenue, Detroit, showed me a clay model of the fighting front up ahead, where our troops were attacking the Japs on mountain ridges on both flanks of the trail.

Our 155 howitzers opened up suddenly from a nearby hillside. Seconds later we heard them hit on Yamashita Ridge, a Jap stronghold, with terrific explosions.

"That's beautiful music," said Samsky, smiling broadly.

A bunch of GI's were standing on the hillside below us,

roaring with fun. I walked down the slope where Sergt. Sam Cotton, of Mason, Mich., was playing with Suzie, a pet monkey he has had for seven months. He caught Suzie in the Leyte campaign and put a small leash on her until she became friendly.

Suzie jumped into his arms, snuggled in the crook of one elbow, and then showed her teeth to a Filipino Joe.

"Suzie hates the Filipinos," Cotton said. "But she's a lot of fun and a lot of company. She sleeps with me at night. When I toss her out of the blankets in the morning, Suzie gets mad and scolds the daylights out of me."

I sat on the hillside awhile with Lieut. Tom J. Cleary, of Cleveland, and Lieut. Clarence N. Kennedy, of LeRoy, N. Y., getting some dope on the campaign.

After the battle of San Manuel, Luzon, where the Japs were given a sound drubbing, they retreated up the trail. The 32nd cut their rear guard to pieces from San Nicolas to Tayug, and then took up the trail.

The "Cat" tractors followed the front line troops, building the supply road with dynamite and bulldozers.

One of them was knocked out by artillery fire and another went over a cliff. The early fighting was for the water points. The Nips would fight hard for one, then retreat to another; finally, they dug in and refused to retreat.

The Nips plastered the Yanks' part of the trail with long range machine guns, 15 guns, 75 mortars, 90 and 150 mm. knee mortars, and 47 mm. artillery field pieces. They attacked our lines at night with sacks of dynamite, shovels and trenching tools in hand-to-hand Banzai attacks.

Japs in the Cacayan valley on the other side moved up to support them. The fighting developed from one hill to another on both sides of the trail.

The Japs used "lunge mines" against the Yanks, long bamboo poles with mines attached to them; they attacked with bayonets on long bamboo poles.

All the Nips carried battle flags wrapped around their abdomens, flags of white with red centers, all bearing the names of relatives written on them.

The Japs covered their foxholes with straw for camouflage.

They dug into caves of four rooms, with manhole entrances, all built on the reverse slopes to escape our artillery. Our artillery made direct hits on them; our troops crept up and tossed dynamite into them.

"These Nips are funny people," said Lieut. Kennedy. "A Jap officer, in white gloves and a long saber, stood on a ridge looking at us. A self-propelled 105 of ours blew him up, and the boys cheered."

I went for a walk on the hill and was lucky to run into Maj.-Gen. W. H. Gill, of Colorado Springs, Col., the division's tough, rugged commander. I told him I was going up to the front.

"It's a little hot up there today," he said. "In fact, every day. Keep your head down."

I got into another jeep and we started for the front.

« 3 »

The Battle for Dog Hill

MAJ.-GEN. W. H. GILL, the fighting commander of this mountain fighting division, told me it was wise to look like a GI at the front.

So I put on my new GI green fatigues, replaced my fatigue cap with a green helmet, pulled on my combat boots, and took off the metal war correspondent's insignia. I filled my canteen from a Lister bag.

Our party climbed into a jeep and we started up the Villa Verde Trail in a broiling sun. Pvt. Theodore E. Metzger, 4973 Cabot avenue, Detroit, was driving, with a Garand rifle in the rack in front of him.

Lieut-Col. Benjamin O. Turnage, of Farmville, N. C., of the 6th Army staff, and Capt. Carl K. Bomburger, Berkeley, Calif., of the division staff, rode with me.

It was a long slow ride. As we came to a four-mile open stretch, with the Japs looking down our throats from Yamashita Ridge and Mt. Imugan, we felt like goldfish in a bowl.

It was comforting to see an M-7, a self-propelled 105, at a turn in the trail, its gun crew giving us cover.

"I'm going to speed up," Pvt. Metzger warned us. "The Nips have made some direct hits on our vehicles along here." We held on.

As we drove we saw a Yank tank that had burned from an artillery hit, and a junk heap that was once one of our radio cars. A Jap infiltration party had destroyed it with a demolition grenade—and then died on the slope.

We drove up to Hill 506, which the Yanks had won after a hard fight, and Pvt. Robert VanderZand, 19230 Blake street, Detroit, a rugged rifleman, was our guide.

We started a climb up a foot path. It seemed like 1,000 yards. Pvt. VanderZand scrambled up like a mountain goat.

My helmet was heavy. I slipped and crawled and hung on to stumps of trees destroyed by artillery fire. I fell once and the Detroit GI grabbed me in the nick of time.

Our party ducked low as we swung out as silhouettes on the ridge line, with the Japs surely watching us from the heights of Hill 507-D.

Finally we reached the crest, and I sat down on the edge of a hole. There was a strong stench and I looked inside at the remains of a Jap soldier. We saw a half dozen dead Japs as we climbed.

Our artillery was booming with the heavy barks of 105's. There was hard fighting on the slope of 507-D, 500 yards away.

Suddenly our machine guns on this hill opened up with bursts of six, then more, then more, endlessly. I crawled over to a forward machine gun position.

There was Pfc. Victor Ostrowski, 9722 Yellowstone avenue, Detroit, pumping his machine gun away at the Japs on Hill 507-D above our troops.

Pfc. Arthur R. Cairo, 13927 Anglin avenue, Detroit, another machine gunner, was banging away with his gun at our left. The machine guns of ours paused for a few moments.

Ostrowski turned and we started talking.

"Those riflemen over there have got it tough," he said. "Imagine climbing up that slope and fighting all the way. It's hard enough just to climb it. A few minutes ago a Nip shell passed over my head, about five feet." He laughed.

He told me Pfc. Loreto A. Cianfarani, 6126 Cadillac avenue, Detroit, a machine gun squad leader, was farther ahead, directing machine gun fire.

I crawled over and talked to Pfc. Cairo, a rugged looking machine gunner, very tanned as the veteran of many campaigns. "We're trying to keep those Nip machine gunners down," he said.

Our machine guns opened up again. I looked through the field glasses that Harry S. Toy, former Michigan Supreme Court jurist, had carried in the last war as a machine gun captain and loaned to me.

Our troops had taken cover on the slope. It was hard to find them at first.

One of them behind a log was shooting with his M-I. Another on his flank was banging away with a tommygun.

Others were crawling and firing. I couldn't see a Jap in my glasses—but they could.

An officer was shouting on our slope to a machine gun crew. "Raise it, damn it all!" he shouted. "Run it across to the left! Let 'em have it!"

"That's fair!" the officer roared again.

"Up, up, up!" he ordered.

Our overhead fire was keeping the Japs on Hill 507-D, called

Dog by our troops who have been fighting for it for 10 days, pinned down.

An officer said the Japs were holed in on the higher slope, on the crest above our boys, and on the reverse slope. They had orders to hold the hill or die.

The machine gun at my left quit firing. A GI jumped up, oblivious to cover, and ran back over the crest.

"Damn it," he said as he ran, "damn it all, a ruptured cartridge!"

An officer jumped up and raced to the machine gun. The crew worked feverishly over it. The GI came running back with a long, thin tool. They got the ruptured cartridge out and renewed firing.

"That's more like it," Machine Gunner Ostrowski growled.

« 4 »

Daredevil Pilot Posts Yanks

THE SUN WAS hot enough to fry eggs at noon and Item and Love companies (military code designations) were fighting down below me on the slope of Hill 507-D.

It was a tough fight, rough enough just climbing the slope, taking all of a veteran rifleman's ingenuity to find cover, requiring split second wariness when the Jap machine guns sprayed their way.

As a civilian in uniform I had a great feeling of pride in these boys. It seemed to me at the time that these Yanks were some of the best troops in the world, and it was amazing that four years ago they were just lads back home without any thought of war.

I found out later from the regimental records that some Detroit boys were out there fighting in the broiling sun. They were Sergt. John M. Sunich, 2161 Anderdon avenue; Pfc. Louis

E. Murray, 1226 Water street; Corp. Aksel Pedersen, 12717 Cheyenne avenue; Pfc. Clayton O. Johnson, 711 Hilldale avenue east, and Pfc. Walter J. Mydlak, Jr., 7511 Prairie avenue.

Watching them through my field glasses, I thought: My gosh, if I ever get back home in Detroit I'll never complain about the rationing of meat points again. It's funny what you think of up front.

But there was another side of war. From my foxhole I looked back down the rear slope of Hill 506, where we were, and saw a group of GI's playing poker in a tunnel. They had been on guard the night before on our perimeter defense.

Somewhere near me I heard a portable radio, and the hollow, deep sound of a radio voice, "Six hundred short . . . deep Jap tunnel . . . some Japs there."

I could hear the Detroit machine gunners ahead of me talking, Pfc. Victor Ostrowski, 9727 Yellowstone avenue; Pfc. Arthur R. Cairo, 13927 Anglin avenue, and Pfc. L. A. Cianfarani, 6126 Cadillac avenue.

"We gotta get that blankety blank hill!" one of them said.

"We sure have," another said. "Remember that stack of mail that just came in and was left when the Nips pushed us off Dog Hill about three weeks ago."

Somebody groaned.

"Cripes," he said, "I hope that mail is still there—when we get there!"

The report was that the Japs had sealed themselves in 21 caves on Dog Hill, and were planning to dig themselves out for a night counter attack, while their machine guns and dug-in riflemen protected them.

A Piper Cub was flying high over us. I saw a lieutenant-colonel sitting with a radio telephone. I crawled over there.

I heard the Piper Cub artillery observer reporting: "holes five zero dog (Hill 507-D) pretty well covered over."

The colonel (and that is what I like about our higher ranking officers—you'll always find them up front with the GI's) was talking to the Piper Cub as it flew over Dog Hill.

"Can you see our own troops, over."

"Say again over," the voice of the Piper Cub replied by radio.

"Can you see our troops, over."

"Haven't picked up any of our troops yet. Wait a minute. Will take a look a little closer, over."

"Roger." (okay).

"Willco." (Will do.)

The Piper Cub swooped low, down to 200 feet, very bravely without armament or anything but Army automatics on the pilot and artillery observer.

"He's my best pilot," the colonel said. "What a flying fool he is." That was the judgment of Lieut.-Col. R. A. Ports of Columbus, O.

"Sometimes the Japs bang away at him, but just keeping him in here will keep their artillery off us."

Pfc. Cairo shouted at me from his sand-bag gun position, "Those Cubs are the infantry's best friend and the Nips' worst enemy." A field piece went off nearby, one of ours. I heard the pilot saying, "I see them all right. Our stuff is going over them okay."

"Keep surveillance if you will," Col. Ports said, "over."

"Roger!"

An infantry captain rushed up out of breath, with an anxious look on his sun-bronzed face.

"What do you want us to do?" asked the colonel. "We'll be glad to do it."

"We want to know if the Japs are coming over the crest of Dog Hill."

The Colonel spoke to the pilot.

"Look over top of 507 Dog. Keep out of way of our mortars. Look see if Japs coming up, over."

"Roger."

The Cub swooped lower. A GI muttered, "My gosh, look at that guy; he's down to 150 feet — or lower."

Then came the pilot's voice, "Two holes right over ridge, Roger."

"Nice work, over."

"Okay, sir, will stay around and look see."

Our mortars opened up on the two holes on the far side of the ridge. I saw the dirt blow up as the mortars hit. I had the feeling that some Nips were joining their Shinto gods.

Our mortars, our artillery, our machine guns opened up. This was real team play, real co-ordination, the Yank Army at work—at its best.

« 5 »

Generals In Fox Holes

WHAT I LIKE about our generals is that they go right up into the front line with our fighting Yanks, unconcerned about personal danger but deeply concerned about how the daily fighting is going.

There are no swivel chair generals in the 32nd Division. I know, for I have seen them at the front, and only the other day a Jap field piece dropped a shell in front of the jeep in which Maj.-Gen. W. H. Gill was riding, blowing the hood off the jeep and putting 20 holes in the jeep's top. But the General was unscathed. A shell fragment scraped the stomach of his aid beside him.

So here I was on Hill 506, watching our troops fighting on Hill 507 Dog. A Detroit GI said to me, "Gen. Lyman is over there, up front a ways."

I started over, at a half-crouch, as the Japs fired two rounds of mortars on us. They had a noisy, whining sound. I dove into what was an empty foxhole and lay doggo. They hit on the forward slope of our hill and threw up a curtain of dirt. As I looked up I found I had two GI riflemen with me.

"That last one sounded a little close," one of them said. He knocked on the wooden stock of his rifle for luck. "Must have thrown a little dirt on the General," he added.

I crawled warily over to where Brig.-Gen. Charles Bishop Lyman, the assistant division commander, was kneeling in a foxhole, watching the action.

Our machine guns opened up with a terrific, staccato sound in the direction of the hidden Jap mortar. Our field artillery laid down a barrage. At my left a GI was digging a deeper foxhole with a pick ax in the broiling sun.

I heard a colonel saying, "If you see a Jap from here, it's rare. They are masters of camouflage."

I shook hands with Gen. Lyman, an Hawaiian and graduate of West Point. We talked for a moment about beautiful Hawaii, where I had been about two weeks ago on my trip out to the Southwest Pacific.

"My middle name is after a fellow named Bishop," Gen. Lyman said. "He did a wonderful thing for Hawaii. He set up a trust fund so Hawaiians could get a college education for only $50 a year."

He scanned the fighting on the slope below. He said our boys had fought their way to within 75 yards of the crest, but he knew the last few yards were always the hardest.

Suddenly he said: "Here it is!"

A Jap machine gun opened up on our observation

post with a blast of fire that sounded like corn popping. Their guns have a lighter firing sound than our machine guns. I dropped flat on my face, ramming my chin on a mess kit.

But the Jap was firing high and his bullets chopped over our heads. All our boys and all our officers were safely down. Then our machine guns drove the Jap gunner to silence.

"Give 'em hell!" the General said.

I looked over on another ridge and saw a patrol slowly climbing it, one of ours, all spread out; their Garands had a business look.

The fighting went on all day. Later I learned our riflemen had fought their way up 35 yards and killed many Japs.

Still later that night Item and Love companies (military code designations) annihilated Jap counter attackers and Gen. Gill's face lit up with pleasure at the news.

On my long slow trip down the ridges of Hill 506 I saw more dead Japs, and noted that most of the trees were skeletons and all the underbrush had been destroyed by our artillery fire.

I met Pvt. William B. Horsey, of Auburn Heights, near Pontiac, Mich., checking our telephone wire. "We have quite a few Nip raids at night," he said, "but I'm dug in pretty deep with sandbags around my foxhole."

Down on the Villa Verde Trail, in the shade of a corner, I saw some GI's reading the Foxhole News, a front line daily newspaper of one sheet, mimeographed on both sides, with the latest war news and the latest news from home.

Down still farther off the trail was—of all things—a Red Cross canteen. I remembered the Red Cross fund campaign just before I left home, and here it was in practicality.

Pfc. Lester L. Fall, of Chesaning, Mich., a former platoon rifleman, was working at this front line canteen, well sandbagged in. There were free cups of coffee and free cigarets.

There were such necessary things up front as shaving brushes and shaving cream and matches—a scarce article out here.

I saw a C-47 dropping parachute supplies of food and ammunition to Filipino guerillas far away on another ridge. My guide, Pvt. Theodore E. Metzger, 4968 Cabot avenue, Detroit, remarked that "the riflemen get a case of beer for every Jap fanatic they catch alive."

In the regimental CP I saw a red chalk sign "The Emperor's birthday is tomorrow!"

I rode back in the jeep to our hillside camp on the Villa Verde Trail.

« 6 »

Yank "Valentines" For Japs

IT WAS VERY COOL on our ridge of the Villa Verde Trail, though the Japs overlooking us on Yamashita Ridge could make it hot enough, as they often did from their higher positions.

I noticed a tension in the air, with staff officers busy on their telephones alerting the division for the night all the way from the foothills in the rear to the forward positions near the Salacsac pass. Everywhere the officers and the GI's were talking about Emperor Hirohito's birthday on the next day (April 29). For our soldiers it held an import of suspense, of coming Jap fanaticism.

Our perimeter defense was tight that night, with our machine gunners in their sandbag positions, an efficient road block to our camp.

"If the Nips come over tonight, they'll get a hot reception," a machine gunner said.

"I think the General's got a little Yank celebration planned anyway," another GI said. "They'll get some valentines from us all right."

The news came in that we had taken Hill 508, after hard fighting up ahead, and everyone was all smiles. The fighting was still sharp on 507-D—Dog Hill.

In our squad tent that night, some of my roommate-officers pushed the safety lock off their 45 automatics, and clicked a bullet into the chamber. GI's did the same with their Garands. We kept our helmets handy below our cots.

At 0001 (one minute after midnight) on the Emperor's birthday I woke up at the terrific din. Our 155 howitzers were sending over those "valentines" to Yamashita Ridge. The firing kept up for hours.

The next day I went over to Batteries B and C of the 121st Field Artillery, where our gunners and our gun crews were working like a super deluxe champion Michigan foot ball team. They all knew it was Hirohito's birthday, and they enjoyed their work all the more.

Pfc. William E. Fleming, of 301 Bayside avenue south, Detroit, drove me over to see the artillery boys. "They sure pounded the hell out of Yamashita Ridge last night and early this morning," he said. "Boy, oh boy, that was a good deal."

I met Pfc. Wayne A. Foster, of Quincy, Mich., who used to work for a Detroit factory as a truck driver. Now he is an assistant gunner of the big howitzer, "Level Bubbles."

"We let go at 0001," he said. "As we threw the first shell in, one of our boys said, 'Here's the first one for the Emp's birthday!'"

He told me they fired till 2 a. m., took a few hours sleep, then threw shells at Yamashita Ridge for hours, starting again at 5 a. m.

Bill Fleming drove me up a steep winding road to the gun position of a howitzer called "The Fighter Third." Pfc. Peter

Centofanti, 3901 McDougall avenue, Detroit, a gunner, grinned over his "birthday fire mission."

"Our observers spotted two big explosions," he said. "We made some direct hits on enemy positions from 14,000 yards Brother, that's shooting!"

Bill Fleming took me to still another gun position, where I shot the breeze with Pvt. Clifford W. Martell, 729 Bundy street east, Flint, Mich.; and Pfc. Robert C. Casmer, of Inkster, Mich., both cannoneers. They said Lieut. George Gregory, of 10385 Morley avenue, Detroit, was up front on one of our hills, as an artillery observer.

"This is the best blankety blank outfit in the whole army," Pvt. Martell said.

"And you can put that to music," remarked Pfc. Casmer.

They summoned Pfc. Casimir J. Burzynski, of 4099 Oliver avenue, Detroit, who has charge of the battery's ammunition, from his squad tent.

"Old Baker Battery is sure plastering the Nips today," Pfc. Burzynski said. "But your ears get you with a helmet on when our howitzer lets go. We don't mind it, though. When we fired practice rounds in garrison we sort of dogged it, you know. But not now. We know every time we fire the piece we kill a lot of Japs. It's about time for another round."

Pfc. Burzynski was quite a prophet. A moment later, an officer with a telephone at his ear shouted briskly, "Battery adjust!"

The gun crew raced to its howitzer on the dead run. It reminded me of Knute Rockne's old hike-hike formations of the Notre Dame backfield shift. These artillery boys sure have a dashing esprit de corps.

The "fire chief" had his left ear to the telephone.

"Left three!" he ordered.

The crew was busy at the gun, more orders, more activity,

like a quarterback calling signals, and the backfield shifting into a double wing back formation of a foot ball team.

"One open, sir, one round!" a voice at the gun said.

The fire chief's right hand was up.

Two loaders with a live shell shouted, "Hike-hike, ready ram!" The shell went home.

The fire chief's right hand did a saber thrust downward in the air. The howitzer roared. It roared again and again. We could hear the big shells exploding far away on Jap-held Yamashita Ridge.

As we drove back to division, Bill Fleming said, "Those battery boys are some stuff, by golly. They give the Japs hell."

And all along our lines that day the Nips were catching hell on Emperor Hirohito's birthday.

« 7 »

Sneak Attack on Hospital

THIS IS THE kind of a story that makes you mad, and it made a lot of our troops fighting mad. Before the day was done the Nips on our front had paid heavily for this atrocity.

For at 6:30 a. m. on Emperor Hirohito's birthday the Nips celebrated their national holiday with a sneak attack on the Red Arrow Division's hospital on the Villa Verde Trail.

They sneaked in two Jap machine guns on the ridge overlooking the hospital, which lies in a little gully just off the trail, beside a cold-water mountain stream.

The machine guns sprayed the hospital's patient-ward tents and the surgical tent. They laid down rounds of fast popping bullets all over the hospital's area. Then the Jap mortars opened up on the hospital. Two mortar shells made a direct hit on an ambulance, well marked with bright Red Crosses. Fortunately it was empty.

Two Yanks wounded in the hard fighting in the mountains were wounded again by the Jap ambushing machine guns.

The Japs tried to wipe out the hospital, its patients, its medical personnel, and its guards of troops. They failed because the ward tents housing the patients are well protected by four feet of sandbags, and the entire hospital has sandbags around its tents, and deep foxholes for protection.

The troops on guard finally drove the Japs off, and our artillery pummeled the ridge, where the Nips had their guns, with a heavy concentration of Yank fire power.

I rode up to the hospital with Maj. Gen. William H. Gill, the tall, lean, taciturn commander of the division. The General was hopping mad as he made the rounds of the hospital. Later, he personally co-ordinated the defense of the hospital, and still later he gave the orders that paid the Japs back tenfold for their hospital attack.

Sergt. Charles E. Kinney, 611 Kitchener avenue, Detroit, drove us in a jeep to the hospital. "Now you know," Sergt. Kinney said, "why our troops hate the Japs so much. The Jap has no respect for the rules of war on medics and the wounded. He would slaughter them all, if he could."

Corp. Clark S. Richmond, 1631 Log Cabin avenue, Detroit, reported that the Jap attack was the third in 10 days on the hospital. "They always open up at 6:30 a. m.," he said. "Just like an alarm clock."

I sat talking about the latest attack, in a squad tent, with Corp. Richmond, Sergt. Ray H. Moerschell, 2946 Anderdon avenue; Sergt. Anthony J. Karath, 736 Solvay avenue north; Sergt. Edmund F. Kupstus, 6417 Walton avenue, and Corp. George H. Neubacher, 6636 Barlum street; all Detroiters.

I asked the $64 question that must be in your minds. Why

wasn't the hospital moved back farther toward the rear after the Nip attacks?

The Detroit medic technicians, trained like a team to tend the wounded under the direction of medical officers with long experience in civilian life as surgeons and doctors, explained that the wounded troops could not stand too long a ride down the dusty, curving, precipitous Villa Verde. They needed short rides, tough enough on them, and quick hospital attention. So the hospital just "sweated out" the Jap attacks.

"The Nips would go after the hospital no matter where we put it," Sergt. Karath said.

All these Detroiters had dropped down behind sandbags as the Jap machine guns opened up, and some of the bullets had come close.

"Tell the folks back home," said Corp. Neubacher, "that the war is over here—except for the fighting."

This portable hospital is the closest operating hospital to the front lines on the Villa Verde. The litter bearers pick up the wounded at the front and carry them to the battalion aid stations, where their wounds are dressed and bandaged, and they are given morphine shots. Then the ambulances bring the wounded a few thousand yards to this hospital.

The wounded are evacuated later to a hospital on the foothills of the Caraballo's, and then taken by Piper Cubs to the big general hospitals far behind the lines in Luzon.

One of the Cubs was donated to the division by the school children of the Hampton Elementary School in Detroit.

Sergt. Ellsworth Bakewell, 1910 Lawndale avenue, Detroit, a surgical technician, showed me a ward tent which was sprayed with holes from mortar shells. A Yank captain and two Filipino supply carriers were lying comfortably on their cots. They had been wounded farther up the trail. Now they were cheerful, looked fine, and were confident of recovery.

We stepped aside as the medics carried a wounded Yank in on a stretcher after an operation. He was heavily bandaged about the abdomen and a medic held a glass jar up high above him while they fed Dextrose into his veins.

Bakewell was still wearing a surgical mask. He had been sleeping in the surgery tent when the Japs opened up. A bullet lodged in a box by his head. He now has the bullet for a souvenir.

Three surgeons work around the clock every day, doing abdominal operations, amputations, and everything but brain surgery.

I met Capt. Philip C. Johnson, the chaplain, who said he had "a beautiful souvenir."

"The Nips put a bullet right into my Bible," he added.

The General talked to the wounded, looked at a Filipino father and son who had been wounded, consulted with the doctors, and again checked the defenses of the hospital.

He walked away to the jeep very grim. He was still hopping mad. Everybody in our jeep, including the General's aide, his machine gunner, the Detroit jeep driver and myself were hopping mad, too.

I was glad to find out later that the Nips paid dearly for this raid.

32nd's Hours of Combat

« 8 »

THE FIGHTING men of the 32nd Division have been slugging it out at point-blank firing range with the Japs for more than three months high in the Caraballo Mountains on the Villa Verde Trail.

This campaign has been one of the division's hardest. The troops have won it despite all hardships of climate, terrain and Jap fanaticism. In the mountain battle they have beaten the Japs at their best.

But there is a reason why our boys are winning on the slopes, in the gullies, on the high ridges, and on the trail itself.

The largest percentage of these troops, the medics who save the wounded, the engineers who build the mountain road, the artillery and mortar men who drive the Japs underground, and the vast number of soldiers who keep the supplies and ammunition, food and water moving up the trail under fire—most of these Red Arrow lads are veterans of 37 months overseas.

On April 22, for example, and that was the date of the division's third anniversary in the Southwest Pacific, the Red Arrow soldiers and officers had experienced 13,030 hours of actual combat, or 543 days.

The division lays claim to "the most combat time of any division in the U. S. Army" in this war.

The American Legion members back home, who fought in World War I with the division in the Aisne-Marne, Meuse-Argonne, Champagne and Aisne-Oise engagements, when the division was the first American division to cross the Hindenburg Line, can be proud of the Red Arrow men of another generation.

For this is a "hot" division in the 6th Army of Gen. MacArthur's forces in the Philippines. Units of the 32nd marched across the terrible Owen Stanley range in New Guinea, and it fought in the mountains of Leyte. Some of the GI's have jokingly remarked that "our insignia ought to be that of a mountain goat!"

Consider this chronology of the Red Arrow Division:

Oct. 15, 1940: Inducted into Federal service.

April 22, 1942: Sailed from San Francisco for the Southwest Pacific.

May 14, 1942: Landed in Adelaide, South Australia.

July 18, 1942: Division moved to Brisbane, Queensland.

Sept. 18, 1942: First elements committed in World War II in New Guinea.

Oct. 11, 1942: 126th Infantry, 2nd Battalion, began the long march across the Owen Stanley range.

Nov. 9-11, 1942: 126th Infantry flown to Pongani.

Jan. 22, 1943: Buna-Sanananda campaign completed.

April 8, 1943: Division completed movement to Australia.

Sept. 4, 1943: Division began movement to New Guinea for the second time.

Jan. 2, 1944: 126th regimental combat team landed at Saidor.

April 22, 1944: 127th RCT took part in Altapo landing.

Sept. 15, 1944: 126th RCT took part in Morotai landing.

Nov. 14, 1944: 32nd arrived at Leyte.

Nov. 16, 1944: Red Arrow committed at Leyte.

Jan. 27, 1945: 32nd landed on Luzon.

Jan. 30, 1945: Division committed in 1st Corps on Luzon.

There were many Detroit and Michigan men fighting in these campaigns with the Red Arrow. Most are now going into their fourth year of overseas duty.

Men like Corp. Lester J. Mack, 5043 Marlborough, Detroit; Sergt. Anthony Piskorski, 2311 Danforth street, Hamtramck; Pfc. Leo J. Gagnon, 65 Inches street, Mt. Clemens; Sergt. Robert M. Lovell, Leonard, Mich.; Sergt. Henry Domanowski, 3880 Yemans avenue, Hamtramck.

All these men are bronzed from the tropical sun, lean and hard and rugged from the outdoor life in the jungles and mountain ranges.

Soldiers like Corp. Thaddeus Rejewski, 13036 Mitchell street, Detroit; Sergt. Richard E. Simpson, 12348 Corbett street, Detroit; Corp. Emil S. Magler, 5633 Martin avenue. Detroit; Pfc. Sidney E. Frankhouse, 523 Fourth street west, Monroe, Mich.; Corp. Peter J. Hegyi, 8824 Witt street, Detroit.

Most of these Michigan fighting men have won the American Defense ribbon, the Asiatic Pacific Theater ribbon with stars, the Good Conduct medal, the Philippine Liberation ribbon with stars, and some have been in companies and regiments that have won the Presidential Unit Citation.

Other three-year overseas veterans are: Sergt. Edmund W. Wojtowicz, 9114 Keller avenue, Detroit; Sergt. Frank W. Kimmel, 6245 Helen avenue, Detroit; Corp. Dominic Vallone, 3510 Sheridan avenue, Detroit.

Pfc. Thomas H. Kochanek, 9519 Graham avenue, Detroit; Corp. Donald D. Rolph, of Pollman, Mich.; Sergt. Andrew J. Heck, 125 Haltiner street, River Rouge; Pvt. Rex W. Castle, who worked at Kelsey Hayes Wheel Co. in Detroit as a spot welder; Sergt. Anthony Vocina, 44 Henry street, River Rouge.

Our front line troops like the medics, who brave enemy machine gun fire and mortars, and Jap suicidal infiltration squads, to save the wounded every hour of the war.

In the 107th Medical Battalion there is a compact little group of Michigan men who are doing a grand job. They include:

Sergt. Alfred C. Ruthowski, 7020 Sarena avenue, Detroit; Sergt. Joseph A. Turowski, 8551 Kenny avenue, Detroit; Pfc. Oscar F. Stoelt, 824 Forest street, Wyandotte; Sergt. Clayton F. Mitchell, 2253 Ninth street, Wyandotte; Sergt. Francis B. Kenny, 335 Walnut street, Wyandotte; Sergt. Joseph Biebel, 2826 Third street, Wyandotte; Pfc. John J. Scott, 12 Applegrove street, Ecorse, and Pfc. Barney J. Bozymowski, 893 Vinewood avenue, Wyandotte.

Then there are replacements like Pvt. Victor Telban, 8226 Ashton street, Detroit, who joined the division recently and felt right at home with all the Michigan veterans.

Some of the Michigan men this month have received awards for heroic service in action.

Staff Sergt. George T. Tulauskas, 793 Channing avenue, Ferndale, a medic, was awarded the Bronze Star for "heroic achievement" in treating and evacuating wounded under enemy artillery fire.

The citation approved by Maj.-Gen. William H. Gill, division commander, said that "without regard for his personal safety, Sergt. Tulauskas showed exceptional courage by exposing himself to this danger, administering first aid to the wounded and directing the evacuation of severely wounded casualties."

This Ferndale sergeant is a lot of soldier. He is now in action high in the Caraballo Mountains, although he won his award near Capocan, on Leyte.

Staff Sergt. Charles F. Zukowski, 7234 Miller street, Detroit, recently won the Bronze Star for meritorious achievement in military operations against the enemy on Luzon.

Four Detroit soldiers have just received Purple Hearts for wounds received on Luzon. Their folks will be glad to know they are fully recovered and back with their units.

They include Pfc. John M. Sutton, 9276 Burt road, a rifleman; Sergt. Herman G. Fritz, 13319 Prest street, a squad leader of riflemen; Sergt. Charles T. Follette, 18894 Greeley street, another squad leader; and Sergt. David C. Hamm, 25 Margaret street east, Detroit, who won the oak leaf cluster to his Purple Heart.

Some of our Michigan boys received hard-won promotions the other day, including Pfc. Milford D. Sylvester, 17445 O'Connor street, Allen Park, a Purple Heart award winner, who was jumped to a staff sergeant as a squad leader of riflemen fighting on the Villa Verde Trail.

Others were Corp. Robert H. Miley, 809 Kales Building, Detroit, advanced to a sergeant with the medics; Corp. H. Carl Ammon, 26976 Westland road, Detroit, promoted to a sergeant, and Corp. William M. Kohler, 420 Osmun street, Pontiac, advanced to a sergeant with his signal company.

The other day the Commonwealth Government of the Philippines awarded the Philippine Liberation medal to Pfc. Wilfred S. Bastow, Auburn Heights, Mich., and to Pvt. William E. McVity, of Falmouth, Mich., who is a member of a field artillery battalion.

« 9 »

The Laughing General

HAVE YOU EVER wondered what a division commander, who is like a general manager of a war production plant back home in the sense that he "runs the works," does up in the front lines?

I rode up to the front one day with Maj.-Gen. William H. Gill, commander of the Red Arrow Division, spending eight hours with him on the Villa Verde Trail, 6,000 feet high in the Caraballo Mountains.

Gen. Gill has all-seeing eyes that took in the vast panorama of fighting on the Villa Verde. Nothing escaped him. He had a sharp eye for little details that decide whether our platoons will lick the Japs on the hillside.

With utter disregard for his personal safety (and he has narrowly escaped injury or death in four previous inspections on the Villa Verde), the General roamed all over our positions on the trail.

He climbed up the steep slopes of Hill 506 and watched our troops on Hill 507 Dog repel a sharp enemy counterattack in mid-afternoon.

As I rode up in the jeep with him, I could not help thinking what a Michigan soldier had told me a few days before.

"The General is a good friend of the GI's" said Corp. Chetney Lee Stader, of 1085 LaSalle avenue, Pontiac. "He likes the enlisted men."

Gen. Gill is 59 years old, born in Unison, Va.; an Army officer for 33 years, a battalion commander in the Meuse-Argonne offensive of the last war, when he won the Silver Star; former executive officer and instructor in the Army War College.

The General is a lean, tall, soldierly looking officer, with a bronzed face from leading the division at Saidor and Aitape, in New Guinea, and in the Leyte and Luzon campaigns in the Philippines. He won the Silver Star oak leaf cluster in the Leyte campaign.

We went up to the front with Sergt. Charles E. Kinney, 611 Kitchener avenue, Detroit, driving the jeep; Corp. John J. Andzulewicz, of Cleveland, holding a tommy gun, and Lieut. Clarence M. Kennedy of LeRoy, N. Y., the General's aid, keeping a sharp eye on Jap-held ridges overlooking our trail.

Gen. Gill has been doing a lot of mountain fighting in these campaigns, and his big ambition is to meet the Japs on open ground. We stopped while the General talked to an infantry major.

"We had a little music last night," the major reported.

"They threw some hand grenades and gave us some machine gun fire."

Some rugged-looking infantrymen were in their foxholes, and the General remarked, with glowing pride in his voice, that "looking at them you'll get the reason there are no fat boys in the division."

Our jeep climbed up 1,000 feet to an observation post. The Japs were 2,000 feet away on a higher ridge. As they stuck their heads up, our heavy machine guns sprayed them. The Japs on the ridge were commanded by a Col. Mine, so fittingly pronounced Meany.

Some of our officers were sitting under a canvas cover, looking at the Japs with field glasses as the Yank machine guns opened up with a sound like a pneumatic drill.

The General conferred with his battalion and regimental commanders, hearing their problems first hand and making spontaneous suggestions in a soft, authoritative voice. After listening to these talks you knew this General knew his stuff.

We got in and out of the jeep about 50 times, following the General in his quick, long strides. Everywhere GI's smiled recognition. They like to see their General at the front and they know how often he goes—every day!

On one long ride up the trail, the General watched the smoke of a fire burning on the trail in our lines. He talked to Lieut.-Col. Frank W. Murphy, of Scottsville, Pa., a regimental "exec," and the fire was put out. It was just a little detail, but the General knew it could be seen for miles and might draw Jap artillery fire.

At the portable hospital he stopped before a line of GI's with their feet in their helmets in a solution. He looked at their feet. One GI held up an infected finger and Gen. Gill looked at it carefully.

"I'm okay, sir," the rifleman said. "The darned finger just keeps swelling up. I'm glad it's on my left hand, sir." The General laughed and the GI joined him. It was good to hear them laugh in all the hubbub of our artillery fire power.

We kept driving up forward. Getting out, Gen. Gill walked along a footpath, and an infantryman walked by with an open package under his arm, with a glass container packed in cotton.

"What have you got there, soldier, something good?" the General inquired.

"My favorite chicken soup from my girl back home, sir," the GI said, holding up the quart jar of soup.

"That's the kind of a girl to have," Gen. Gill said.

Our party met Maj. Paul J. Pernish, of 715 Ash street, Owosso, Mich., the leader of a battalion of guerillas. We climbed up on a hill, and watched a Yank patrol of 10 men slowly climbing up the steep slopes of a high ridge, still held by the Japs. The General watched the patrol through a battalion commander's telescope.

I took a look-see, watching a rifleman standing behind a small tree on the slope, peering carefully around, on the alert for a Nip machine gun. They are always around.

I saw riflemen crawl up to a log and lie down behind it. The sun was at foundry heat and the patrol had a four-hour climb ahead of it.

The patrol was moving up to evacuate the body of a dead Yank lying high up on the slope. Two Jap bodies lay nearby, but the Japs never make any effort to bury their dead at the front.

They are different from our boys. Our dead always get the burial that fighting Americans deserve, little graves in Luzon that their bodies make American soil for all time. A little bit of America far from home, these graves.

In the early evening as we drove back down the trail to the General's camp, still not far from the front, our Detroit driver,

Sergt. Kinney, whispered to me, "There's not a place on this trail that is safe from Nip fire."

Lieut. Kennedy remarked, "It was a nice quiet day for a change—the Japs didn't fire at our jeep this time."

But I had been in a few spots where I had ducked instinctively. It didn't seem quiet to me. But, then, I'm just a pencil pusher who is a living example that you can't be scared to death at the front.

« 10 »

Lucky Oddities

A LOT OF Detroit and Michigan soldiers, the fellows you knew back home in civilian life four years ago, do a lot of interesting things on the Villa Verde Trail.

It takes a lot of soldiers, doing all manner of things and having all sorts of experiences, when a division like the Red Arrow is fighting a 24-hour war in the Caraballo Mountains.

Now you take Corp. Raymond C. Richardson, 4611 Moran street, Detroit, a front line medical technician, who had as narrow an escape from death as anyone ever had.

The soldiers are still talking about what happened to Ray. During a fight in a valley, after he had finished bandaging a wounded man, a Jap explosive shell hit only a few yards away from him.

He was knocked down, hit in the chest, thought he was severely wounded and started to diagnose his own case. Much to Ray's surprise he found he was only bruised.

There were only small black and blue marks on his chest and he moved forward immediately. But he left behind him a shell fragment, as large as a man's hand, which had struck him in the chest.

During the hard fighting in the Bailo Mountains of the Villa Verde, four Detroit soldiers dug themselves the latest styles in foxholes.

The Nips poured heavy artillery and mortar fire on their positions. These four Detroiters survived the barrage with something new in foxholes.

They were Sergt. Joseph Pekala, 4822 Renville street; Sergt. Anthony Karoth, 7114 Jefferson avenue west; Sergt. Stanley Zukowski, Jr., 7234 Miller avenue, and Sergt. Stanley Pawles, 6409 Floyd avenue, Detroit.

They dug a small tunnel in the side of a hill and hollowed out a large, roomy compartment—large enough for all four of them to sleep in. Then they dug other hillside "compartments" for the members of their squad.

The main room was used as a dining room, recreation "hall" and bedroom. On a clear day from their tunnel, they could see far away Lingayen Gulf, 30 miles away.

"All the comforts of home," Sergt. Zukowski said, laughing.

Sergt. Thomas S. Raymond, 3380 Piedmore road, Romeo, Mich., is a rugged infantry platoon guide. He has been wounded in action twice, and is still fighting in the Caraballo Mountains, completely recovered.

Sergt. Raymond was wounded first at Buna, recovered, rejoined his platoon. He was wounded the second time at Leyte and is back again in action with more than 500 days of actual combat to his credit. No one soldier could do more.

For wounds received in action in Tayug, in northern Luzon, in the foothills of the Caraballo's, Pfc. Jack C. Sponseller, 611 Beniteau avenue, Detroit, a member of the 107th Medical Battalion, has been awarded the Purple Heart.

Herman is a Leyte monkey who amuses a group of Yanks in their squad tents as a natural "trapeze artist," and Pfc. Paul Jones, 14400 Vassar drive, Detroit, is part owner of Herman.

The monkey, who has become a real pet, cost five pesos ($2.50). Jones owns two pesos and 50 centavos—or one-half of Herman. And Herman's favorite food is shaving soap, served at full lather on a shaving brush.

Corp. Philip Correy, 483 Brainard street, Detroit, and a three-man kitchen crew of the 107th Medical Battalion, recently planned a real anniversary dinner to celebrate their third anniversary overseas with the Red Arrow.

Beginning with cocktails of "Villa Verde Vapor," a favorite GI concoction in Luzon, the menu included fried Luzon chicken, French fried comotes, the anemic looking sweet potato of the Philippines; green peas, hot rolls and butter, strawberry jello and homemade ice cream, with coffee, cigarets and cigars.

It was served on tables with real white table cloths, a grand luxury here.

Some other Detroit boys who are beginning their fourth year's service overseas with the Red Arrow include Pfc. Joseph T. Madey, 1125 Beatrice avenue south, a litter bearer; Pfc. Adam Pawlowski, 3164 Gilbert avenue, a howitzer cannoneer; Corp. Charles N. Mousseau, 550 Dickerson avenue, a medical aid technician.

Pvt. William Hartzog, 14870 Burt road, Detroit, recently completed 24 months of service overseas.

Some day when the division goes to the rear to take a well-earned rest after the Leyte and Luzon campaigns, the information and education section of the Red Arrow is all set up to hold Army Institute classes for the soldiers.

Pvt. John Geyman, 410 Lothrop road, Grosse Pointe Farms, an attorney in civilian life, told me the project was designed to orientate the soldiers for their future re-entry into civilian life. Geyman will teach classes in business law.

Corp. Clark Richmond, of 16328 Log Cabin avenue, Detroit, is alternately the most popular and most unpopular man in the 107th Medical Battalion. As mail clerk, his popularity increases or decreases with the number of "sugar dispatches" from home.

Corp. Walter F. Aherin, who was inducted into service in Detroit after working as a Chrysler welder, is the barber for a quartermaster's company. Walt's specialty is the "Luzon bobtail haircut," done very short with a brush of hair at the top.

Anything can happen on the Luzon front. Pfc. Edward J. Majewski, 8275 Badger avenue, Detroit, hadn't seen his uncle, Pvt. Leo H. Gorecki, 6236 Sheridan avenue, Detroit, for 18 months. They met in a foxhole and are now fighting the Japs side by side.

Pvt. Charles Ray Glisson, 140 Pingree avenue, Detroit, and Pfc. Louis F. De Noble, 1355 Maryland avenue, Grosse Pointe Park, are studying in the Red Arrow's signal company radio school.

The Motor Vehicle Driver's Badge for exemplary performance under fire has been awarded to Corp. Nick Solodky, 318 Lehmann avenue, Hamtramck; Pfc. Renin J. Lanckriet, 4137 Belvidere avenue, Detroit; Pfc. Glenn R. Shepperd, Route 3, Bay City; and to Pvt. Robert D. Helka, 23757 Michigan avenue, Dearborn.

Corp. Peter A. Radigan, 4632 Walwit street, Dearborn, has been awarded the Philippine Liberation Medal by the Commonwealth Government for fighting on Leyte and Luzon.

Pfc. Victor J. Nienartowicz, Route 2, Gaylord, Mich., is with the 107th Medical Battalion.

« 11 »

Time Out For a Slugfest

TWO IGOROTS WERE slugging it out with Yank boxing gloves at the division's cavalry reconnaisance troop's rest camp. Other Igorots stood around in a semi-circle, grinning.

The two boxers threw punches at each other from the hips. They were about five feet tall, rugged, black haired little fellows with flashing black eyes, the fighting hill people of the Philippines, who go out with the cavalry.

The boxers grinned and made chuckling sounds of pleasure as they got hit. They liked hard slugging, close-in fighting.

Others were standing by awaiting their turns to get the gloves on.

Capt. Bernard J. Lillie, of Greenfield, Mass., the troop's commander, stood on the roadside with a large group of men, watching the Igorot boxers with great glee. The Yanks roared encouragement to "mix it."

The troop deserved some laughter. One of its patrols of 30 men was just back from 33 days behind the Jap lines, looking at Baguio, the summer capital, and sitting on the hillside outside Santa Fe, watching Jap troops retreating from the Caraballo mountain ridges.

A larger Jap force had ambushed the patrol in the mountains, and there had been a hot fight. Our boys killed 35 Japs, wounded still more, and drove them off.

I sat around talking to some of the Detroit and Michigan boys in the troop, some who had been on the recent patrol. I met Sergt. Frank J. Tomsej, 13439 Gallagher avenue, Detroit; Corp. Warren W. Blodgett, 657 Scribner street north west,

Grand Rapids, Mich.; Pvt. Sylvester Krupa, 4859 Underwood avenue.

Pvt. Krupa was separated from the patrol in its hot fight and spent two days out in the Jap lines, without water and without food, until he got back safely in our lines.

"I walked up and down so many hills, with the Nips swarming around," he said, "that my natural stance is with one foot in the air."

"It's hard on the nerves, out there alone," Sergt. Tomsej observed.

I missed Corp. Salvatore Comito, 9469 Peter Hunt street, Detroit, who was on a three-day pass to Manila, and Corp. Emmett Kirkwood, 935 Courtney avenue, Grand Rapids, who was out with some Filipino guerillas; and Corp. Thaddeus Ksiazek, 2353 Clark street, Detroit.

Corp. Russel C. Cochrane, of Manton, Mich., a rifleman, gave me their names. "They are rugged gents," he said.

"We walked into ambush over near Timiak, beyond Baguio," Corp. Blodgett said. "They were well camouflaged, lying on both sides of a mountain trail, in the tall kunai grass. We lost six men killed right off the bat. We hit the bush and fought it out. I never saw a Nip. When they fired, we shot them. There were only 30 of us and 100 of them, but we gave them a good licking."

"We got some hot meals up to the boys, breakfast and supper, some days," Tomsej said. "And how we got it there back of the Nip lines is our little secret."

Though the cavalry was originally mechanized, with reconnaissance tanks, armored cars and jeeps with mounted machine guns, the troop now goes into the Jap lines on foot.

Close to the mountain village of Valades, once a headquarters for the guerillas during Jap occupation, one member of the patrol was hit in the knee, and another in the hand in a sharp brush with the Nips.

"We carried the recon guy with the wounded knee out on a stretcher and brought him back to our lines," Blodgett said.

"Once we tried to get into their lines at night," Cochrane said. "The Nips saw us. They worked their way quietly into us. It was so dark you couldn't see your hand in front of you. I shot a Jap officer as he was swinging his saber at one of our boys."

"I helped carry out three of our wounded," Blodgett said. "We had to fight our way in to get them."

Tomsej said the troop walked 8 to 15 hours a day with packs on its patrols.

They recalled that one night they went out on patrol, crept up on a ridge to harass the Japs, killed two of them, drove others into caves, and then crept down the hill as the Japs laid down mortars on them.

"Our Garands flattened some of them, though," Blodgett said. "Our boys fire them so fast they sound like machine guns."

Two Jap companies were occupying a hill off the Villa Verde, and a recon patrol crept up on them, just seven Yanks. "They were all eating dinner," Pvt. Krupa said. "We spread out in a line and opened fire together. We knocked off a lot of them. Most of them dived for their caves.

"Then they started to counterattack. The hill seemed full of Japs. It took nine hours to crawl up to their positions—and 30 minutes to get back!"

« 12 »

A Laugh On the Japs

WE WERE SITTING in the shade of a Nipa thatched hut, and some Michigan boys were talking about those 33 days out on patrol behind the Jap lines.

We were getting ready to make a radio broadcast from Manila, back to radio station WWJ-The Detroit News, and we were sort of rehearsing our material.

"All I ask," said Sergt. Frank J. Tomsej, 13439 Gallagher avenue, Detroit, "is that you don't make a bunch of heroes out of us. These infantry fellows in the mountain front lines are the real heroes."

Corp. Warren W. Blodgett, 657 Scribner avenue, Grand Rapids, Mich.; Sergt. Wallace J. Erickson, of Sparta, Wis.; and Sergt. Raymond W. Tenedine, Ansonia, Conn., were sitting there talking, taking a few sips out of hot canteens now and then.

We had sent a jeep out to get Pvt. Sylvester Krupa, 4859 Underwood avenue, Detroit, who was somewhere up the Villa Verde trail.

Thirty of the recon troop, out on patrol, had been sitting on a hillside while our troops were still driving through the mountains toward it, watching the Japs.

"We were out ahead of the division," said Blodgett. "We were only out 33 days, but it seemed like a hundred when the tension was on."

The troop, by the way, was about 20 miles away from various converging Yank forces in the mountains.

"You guys were almost in the Jap bivouac area, weren't you?" Tomsej asked.

49

"Oh, yes," said Blodgett. "We watched the Nips shaking husks from their rice, and taking baths in the creek. We saw a bunch of them come out one morning and all bow to the sun. A Nip officer came riding up on a horse.

"At dusk they would come out of the bush on the hills, and start to move back. They all looked scared when our artillery would open up on them. We weren't out there, you know, just for a pleasure trip. We could hear our artillery on our radio, 'Ready! Ready! Fire!' Then over would come the shells. Some of those Nippos ran a mile in nothing flat. Our artillery fire got a lot of them."

"It was fun watching our air strikes," said Tomsej. "Our fliers would bomb the Nips and strafe them on the roads."

All the boys started laughing at one time.

"Hey, guys," said Sergt. Tenedine, "remember those Nippo officers?"

Some high Jap officers had come up in a staff car, while the recon troops were sitting in the tall kunai grass above them, watching, observing, like all-seeing eye troops.

The Jap officers all wore white gloves. They had brief cases. They wore shining boots and some of them reached down and dusted off their boots with white handkerchiefs.

"Gee whiz," said Blodgett, "they were a bunch of fancy Dans, and old Krupe (Pvt. Krupa) said, 'We ought to knock off those fancy-looking guys. They must be up to something.'"

Well, our boys weren't just sitting on the hillside for fun. A barrage of Yank shells started coming over. Some of the Japs were hit.

"Then we almost busted a lung up there laughing," said Sergt. Erickson. "Some of those fancy fellows ran down to a deep creek. They held their noses—and jumped in. What a sight! And Tokyo Rose says they're such heroes!"

Our boys ran out of water. They dipped their canteens in a creek, and put in a lot of Halazone tablets to take the germs out of the water. They ate K rations till they ran out, and then ate two comotes (something like a big sweet potato) a day.

Three Japs later came up on another trail and set up a machine gun. Our boys opened fire.

The veteran recon troops started to laugh again. It was enthusiastic laughter. I thought they would split their sides.

"The funniest thing yet happened out there," Blodgett said. "The Nips pinned a piece of white paper on a tree trunk. It said: 'Yank, when are you going home? We have you surrounded!'"

(Blodgett has the Purple Heart; he was shot in the left arm in the Leyte campaign, and recovered.)

"That was a laugh," Tomsej said, "because our boys got back to our lines—a little thinner, awfully tired, but they got back."

"Just a bunch of billy goats in the recon," Blodgett said.

« 13 »

Forward on Hands and Knees

EVERY LINE regiment has its scouts, called the I & R platoon by the military, and they are picked fighting men who do the most amazing things as routine, all in the day's work.

They are tough, hard-going soldiers, who go out on patrols on the hillsides and on the mountain ridges long before we have taken them, and often they slug it out with any Nips they collide with.

The Yanks didn't have high Hill 517 when I went up the Villa Verde Trail, and sat in a dark, sandbagged hillside shelter, talking with some of the regimental scouts of the 127th Regiment.

Lieut. W. B. Crabbe, who was educated in Lansing and whose father lives at 2001 Center avenue, Bay City, led a patrol of seven Yanks and two Igorots, the fighting hill people of the Philippines, in a patrol which spent two days on Hill 517.

Sergt. Carlton S. Beckman, of White Cloud, Mich., and Pfc. Anthony J. Hrydziuszko, 18711 Syracuse avenue, Detroit, were members of the scouting party.

When the patrol started out for Hill 517, it knew it "couldn't go out without being seen by the Nips." For three hours it slowly climbed up 1,000 feet, crawling along at five-yard intervals, till it reached the crest, at an elevation of 4,600 feet.

Hrydziuszko remarked that "half the time I was crawling up that damned hill on all fours. When we got to the top there was real thick bamboo into which the Japs had cut a trail. We were constantly in danger of being ambushed."

"That is a constant strain on the men," Lieut. Crabbe said.

One of our attack bombers had dropped a bomb in this area, clearing out an open space. The patrol ran head-on into three Jap riflemen there.

"We saw them first," Sergt. Beckman said, "and there were three dead Nips in short order, whoops!"

"I got a shot in," said Tony.

Then the patrol reached some Jap caves on the far slope and Lieut. Crabbe said, "There was a beautiful sight."

"Our mortars and artillery had caught about 100 Japs," he said, "and all over the hill were arms and legs and heads of dead Nips. We counted about 100 heads.

"Those are some Nips our infantry—and they really are guys who take it and give it out—won't have to dig out. I guess our heavy stuff caught them flat-footed outside their caves all right."

For no apparent reason, Tony said suddenly, "You know, I miss H. C. L. Jackson's column in The News. I always read him back home."

Then we continued talking about the patrol on Hill 517. It ran into two more Japs and killed them with rifle fire.

Whereupon the gallant patrol swung around, infiltrated back of the Jap lines and watched the foe from 50 feet away in their caves.

These scouts weren't out on the Jap-held hill, of course, just for a long hike. They got what they wanted and they radioed the dope back. Long after they had pulled away from the Jap caves our artillery was zeroed into them.

On this patrol, our boys were carrying two canteens of chlorinated water. They ran out going up and down the hill. Once they saw water down 1,000 yards on a steep cliff. It would have taken a day to get there and back, so they went without water.

"I saw one little wet spot on the trail," Tony said. "I tried to figure a way to drain it—and a guy is really thirsty when he's thinking like that."

They called Sergt. Beckman, "Beck," and he recalled a tough patrol-fight on Leyte when the scouts went in and evacuated some wounded Yanks, carrying them back to our lines.

"Gen. Gill said, 'Crabbe, you get those men out,'" Lieut. Crabbe recalled. "The Japs had ambushed some of our men with machine guns. We went in after them. There were 12 of us. We ran into 18 Japs.

"We killed two, wounded six and drove 10 off. Then about 150 of them came after us. We backed out and got a self-propelled 105 on the beam. The Japs were laid out near some trees, and our 105 blasted them out. The next day we found

10 dead bodies and bloody bandages all over the Jap positions and a knocked-out machine gun."

Beckman won the Bronze Star in that Leyte campaign, and Crabbe won the Silver Star for knocking out a machine gun at Leyte. Beckman has been on 100 patrols in Luzon, Tony on 40 and Crabbe on about 125, they said.

On one of their scouting expeditions with 15 men, they killed 65 Japs in a hard fight in which they lost three men. In the New Guinea campaign, Lieut. Crabbe led a patrol back of the Jap lines, tacking leaflets on the trees demanding the Japs' surrender.

The regimental commander wanted to make an officer out of Beck, but the Michigan sergeant declined and the colonel understood. "This work gets in your blood," Beck said.

On mountain patrols, the scouts have had close calls from their own artillery fire. They told a story about a Yank scout called Popo who ran their short wave radio under mortar fire from our side.

"Hey," Popo yelled over the radio to the mortar section, "quit throwin' your mortars at us, you goons."

But no one was hit and days later they talked about it, as if it was a huge joke.

One Jap almost got all three of them in the mountains a few days ago. He opened up from ambush. The Yank next to the sergeant said, "Beck, I'm hit in the chest."

Beck grabbed him as he started to fall over the cliff. Beck tottered. Tony grabbed him by the seat of the pants, and Lieut. Crabbe killed the Jap. The three of them carried the wounded scout back to our lines.

That's the kind of fighting men, roughnecks all, these Yank scouts are!

« 14 »

I Take a Tumble

A NEWSPAPER GUY can make mistakes, and for days your war correspondent was very uncomfortable when he sat down, all because he got tied up with the regimental scouts on the Villa Verde Trail.

I had been talking to them about their fearless patrols out on Jap-held mountain ridges, talking with Lieut. William B. Crabbe, of Bay City, their leader; Sergt. Carlton S. Beckman, of White Cloud, Mich.; and Pfc. Anthony J. Hrydziuszko, of 18711 Syracuse avenue, Detroit.

"How would you like to watch one of our patrols right now —through a captured Jap telescope?" Tony asked.

That seemed intriguing. We looked down the winding 8-foot wide road the engineers had built under fire on the trail. It curved around in a double S.

"I'm not going to walk all the way down the road where we got that Nip telescope set up," Beck said. "Let's take a short cut."

They walked over toward the steep slope. It looked like a drop off a roller coaster, and I balked.

"Oh, it's a cinch," Lieut. Crabbe said, "Come on!"

They started down and I followed them slowly, slipped, and hung on to a tree root. They went down like a trio of mountain goats, laughing and poking. "Hey, come on!" roared Tony.

So I started down in my new combat boots that were slippery and were putting blisters on my feet. Suddenly, my feet went out from under me. I started down the hill on my posterior at the speed of an express train.

"Keep your hands up; keep your feet up!" Crabbe roared.

The GI's down below on the road were laughing. It was like a few feet out of a Hollywood comic, sliding down the dirt on that hill and breaking all records for sliding. It was like a baseball player sliding from home plate to the center-field flag at Briggs Stadium back home.

Trucks and jeeps were roaring down the road and I was headed for them when Crabbe made a football player's dive, grabbed me by the feet and ended the longest slide on Luzon. Well, my brand new green GI fatigues were well broken in.

"Brother," said Tony, "you sure were a pretty sight coming down that hill. You've got a new technique."

Well, we all laughed, and a lot of GI's joined up, and a big rugged Texan slapped me on the back. "You've been initiated," he said. "You'll learn to stay away from these crazy guys in Crabbe's platoon!"

We walked over to Lieut. Crabbe's hillside cave, with its printed sign, "Jap Opium Den!" They gave me a drink of lukewarm water. Then we walked down to the telescope set up on the edge of a cliff.

For an hour I watched one of our patrols climbing up another Jap-held ridge. You could see the perspiration on their foreheads when they turned around in the sun, so powerful was the telescope.

"Now you know what good equipment those Nips have," Crabbe said. "They use these jiggers to look down our tonsils from those high ridges over there."

"I bet some blankety blank Nip officer in white gloves is looking at us now," Beck said.

The conversation churned about the Nips. These Michigan boys told about finding a Filipino shack up in the hills. They found a Filipino tied to a chair, his hands bound behind him, bayoneted to death. Inside they found an entire family, father and mother and four children, all bayoneted to death.

"What got me," said Tony, "was that little baby in the woman's arms."

"Well, we got four of them a few minutes later," Beck said.

The Japs were roasting a pig on a spit; one of them was behind a tree. Our boys killed the first three, still mad over the Filipino dead at the shack. The Jap behind the tree opened up on them.

"I fired on one side of the tree," Tony said, "and Beck fired on the other side. Pretty soon the Nip fell over backwards, deader than a mackerel."

I told them they were doing one sweet job on the Villa Verde Trail, and Lieut. Crabbe just stared back.

"It's the infantry in the line that does the job, fellow," he said. "What a bunch of guys they are. At Leyte in the Ormoc corridor 10 Jap tanks hit the infantry. A bazooka man knocked off one. Then those riflemen jumped off a ledge, right on top of the tanks, pried open tank hatches and killed the crews with hand grenades."

"What a bunch of guys!" said Tony.

« 15 »

The Sergeant Gets the Beer

THIS IS ONE of those amusing stories that sometimes come out of war, of how Sergt. Willie Brown, of DeWitt, Ark., won a case of beer and a three-day trip to Manila—on a mountain hillside.

To understand how all this could happen, you must first understand Sergt. Willie Brown. They call him The Old Sarge in his company though he is not old.

And Willie is not always a sergeant. He is not much of a garrison soldier, and Willie is always being busted to a buck private when the 32nd is in a rest area. Willie, you see, is a two-bottle man who hates routine and garrison regulations.

As soon as Willie gets to the front, and he has been through seven major campaigns with the Red Arrow Division, he always wins back his sergeant's stripes. Because Sergt. Brown is one of the best front-line platoon sergeants in the Southwest Pacific and a rough, tireless, first-class fighting man.

Now that you have been properly introduced to Willie, you will want to know how he won the case of beer and the three-day pass to the shell-torn, wrecked metropolis of the Orient.

Well, the manner of it was this:

Willie had been leading his platoon of riflemen all day out on a mountainside off the Villa Verde, mopping up Japs hiding in caves. They had killed a lot of Japs. The sun was at its roasting heat. Willie was tired and in need of shade.

The fighting platoon had flushed 20 Japs out of the last cave, and killed them all in a fast, sharp action. Willie thought the box-score was pretty good. So he put his heavy Garand up against the cave, strolled in, and sat down on his helmet.

The cave was dark. Willie sat there for a few minutes, thinking of the laurels to be won by capturing a Jap—a case of beer and a pass to Manila. (The Division has taken 25 Japs in 100 days of fighting in the mountains, and killed more than 7,000.)

Willie has an old soldier's love for beer. As his eyes became accustomed to the cave's darkness, Willie suddenly came out of his reveries. Before him, not five feet away, lay a Jap.

"Ah, ha," said The Old Sarge, "a dead Nippo." But he pulled out his trench knife just to be on the safe side.

Willie bent over the Jap, and put a finger on the veins of his neck. He noted a strong heart beat. "Ah, ha," said Willie Brown, "here is a case of beer and a three-day pass to Manila!"

Willie dug the Jap in the ribs. No movement. The Jap's eyes were closed very tightly.

Willie playfully pinched the Nippo in one leg. The Jap opened one eye, closed it. Willie pinched him in the other leg; The Nip opened his other eye, promptly closed it.

"So you're playing doggo on me!" roared The Old Sarge, turning the Jap over on his back. "You speak good old American?"

The Jap opened his eyes and shook his head.

"You are full of dehydrated spuds," said Sergt. Willie. "Get up. You might as well surrender, Bud."

The Jap came to life. He pointed and grunted at the hand grenades hooked to Willie's cartridge belt.

"Oh," said Willie, "so you want to commit suicide, like all you Nips when you're cornered. No dice, pal, you're a case of beer now, not a Jap."

Willie decided to be a diplomat, though it was hardly in his line. The Nip looked like he hadn't eaten for days. Willie fished out a piece of chocolate, a leftover from a K ration, and handed it to the Jap. The Nip ate it hungrily. Willie gave him a drink out of his canteen, a long drink.

"I bet I get you, Nippo baby," said Willie. "But if you try any monkey stuff I'll cut your gizzard out."

Willie lit a cigaret. The Jap watched him with greedy eyes. Willie gave him a lighted cigaret, and the Nip smiled. Willie offered him another drink of water. The Jap signaled for Willie to drink first. They had a drink together.

"Come on now, Nippo, and surrender; you haven't got a chance," said Willie. "Come on, old boy, and surrender for Willie!"

The Jap stared at Willie a long time, and nodded. Willie glowed with glee.

"You got any grenades?" Willie demanded, and showed him one. The Jap reached under him and handed Willie two grenades. The Jap shook his head sadly.

"You haven't got enough courage to knock yourself off,"

Willie said, and handed him his trench knife with the point still in Willie's hand.

"No, no, no," the Jap said.

Then the Jap handed over his rifle and a saber. Willie got him to his feet and took him out of the cave.

"Hey, fellows," shouted Willie Brown, "lookee what I got—a case of beer and a three-day pass to Manila!"

The Old Sarge led his prisoner away.

« 16 »

A Senseless Banzai Charge

THE JAPS HIT the battalion's perimeter defense at 1:30 a. m., shouting like madmen in a head-on Banzai attack, sometimes shouting in English, "Hay, Mike . . . Hay, Joe . . . you die now!"

It was one of those mountain nights, no moon, the darkness like a shroud, so that Yank riflemen couldn't see one another a few feet away.

But when the Japs hit the riflemen were in their foxholes, the machine gunners were ready, for no one sleeps at night near the Jap lines anyway.

The Japs came on in force. They broke through the perimeter defense for 20 yards. The battalion fought them hand to hand, with trench knives, with bayonets, with anything. Corporals with tommy guns cut down Jap officers with chopping sabers.

For two hours the fight went on, there in the darkness. Then the Japs left 24 dead behind in the battalion's positions, and 15 down the slope, almost dead. Many more were wounded.

Lieut. Col. Douglas E. Des Rosier, 1675 Webb avenue, Detroit, who got a lot of military training in the old National Guard armory back home, commanded the battalion.

"The Japs came out of their spider holes — mountainside caves with four or five entrances, and charged us," Des Rosier said.

"It was one of those mad, senseless attacks they sometimes make. The Banzai attack had momentum, and it carried 'em into our lines for awhile. But we quickly swung our positions around, and drove them out. We had been fighting the Nips for 25 straight days and nights in the Caraballos and we knew how to handle them."

I sat down under a tree, later, talking to a group of Michigan men who had fought through that action.

They were Pfc. Frank S. Tyler, 17540 Keeler avenue, Detroit, a rifleman; Pfc. Linford A. Pease, of Williamston, Mich., a mortar man; Sergt. Clifford J. MacMillan, of Fenton, Mich., mortar man, and Sergt. Bernard J. Tibble, 10640 Gratiot avenue, Detroit, leader of a machine gun squad.

"They hit us with rounds and rounds of artillery and mortars," Sergt. MacMillan said.

"And then they made their rush," added Pfc. Tyler. "My gosh, they made a lot of noise."

"We have some Joe's and some Mike's in our outfit," said Sergt. Tibble. "They got a boot out of hearing those Nips yelling their names."

While we were talking some other Michigan soldiers came up, others who had not been in this particular action. They sat around listening, a highly technical audience.

Among them were Pvt. William F. Crane, 2943 Doris avenue, Detroit, an automatic weaponsman; Pvt. Robert A. Klann, 10710 East Outer drive, Detroit, a litter bearer; Pvt. Arnold L. Hahn, of Unionville, Mich., a rifleman; Pvt. Donald

B. Waters, 925 Ann street east, Ann Arbor, rifleman, and Pvt. Carl A. Hall, Port Huron, rifleman.

"You guys must have had a wild time that night," Pvt. Crane said.

"You can say that again," Pfc. Tyler added. "Some of those Nips yelled, 'Artillery fire. Your area. Move off of this, Joe.' But we didn't fall for that guff."

After the Japs had fought their way into the battalion's perimeter, they dug in. Col. Des Rosier swung platoons around on their flanks. Our machine guns chopped into them from three sides. Our artillery's counter battery fire silenced the Jap artillery. Our mortars poured round after round behind the Japs to prevent reinforcements from coming up.

Some of our boys, of course, were cut off up ahead, but they kept on fighting in their foxholes. They wouldn't quit. Japs jumped in on them, and they fought it out.

"I had a funny feeling," Tyler said. "I had to move into a foxhole, when we attacked, where there had been a direct hit."

"While their mortars were pounding us with about 1,000 rounds," said Pease, "I counted 17 that hit around me. But I was dug in—but plenty."

Finally, Col. Des Rosier gave the order to attack the center and the flanks. The Japs made a stand, but they were slowly driven out. With the perimeter outer defenses re-won, the battalion dug in again for the night.

Our artillery pounded the Japs all night long.

"There is no sweeter music," said Pease.

« 17 »

Planting TNT In A Cave of Japs

I was sitting outside a tent overlooking the shallow Anonas River in Northern Luzon. Some GIs were swimming in the cool, waist-deep river; some were doing their laundry, Filipino fashion, by hitting it with small paddles.

Lieut.-Col. Douglas E. Des Rosier, 1675 Webb avenue, Detroit, the battalion's commander, and Warrant Officer Keith W. (Bill) Agy, 5302 Crane avenue, Detroit, assistant regimental supply officer, were talking about the battalion's 25 days in the mountain front lines.

Bill Agy, now 37 months overseas, had been doing a great job getting supplies far up to the front on the Villa Verde Trail. But Agy is a good shot, too. When snipers fired on his convoy, Bill opened up, firing at 500 yards with a telescopic sight on his Garand.

"It's a lot of fun knocking off a Jap sniper," he said.

Near us, Pvt. Delmar E. Brown, of Laingsburg, Mich., and Pfc. Willard N. Kaiser, 4757 Sheridan avenue, Detroit, were washing their Army clothes in the river. I saw Pfc. Uliphino Carrion, 1104 Warren avenue west, Detroit, and Pvt. William F. Crane, 2943 Doris avenue, Detroit, cleaning their Garands with great care.

Not far away there was the noisy, boisterous laughter of a rhum game in the open, played on a GI blanket, by Sergt. Clifford MacMillan, of Fenton; Sergt. Bernard J. Tibble, 10640 Gratiot avenue, Detroit; Pfc. Frank S. Tyler, 17540 Keeler avenue, Detroit, and Pvt. Charles E. Allgood, 4268 Ninth street, Ecorse, Mich.

Col. Des Rosier and Agy started talking "about the most dangerous job in the Army."

"Those assault men are well trained," Agy said.

"They have to be," said Col. Des Rosier. "They lay those 'family size' demolition charges of 18 pounds into Jap caves. They creep right up to a cave, covered by riflemen and machine guns and plant their charges. I take my hat off to those boys."

"You ought to talk to Lieut. Sakus," Agy said. "He's the limit. He loves that kind of work. I've seen him crawl up to a Jap cave, with six Yanks and five guerillas protecting him, and throw a smoke grenade into a cave that killed 11 Japs."

"I think the only reason he doesn't get hit is that he doesn't care," said Col. Des Rosier.

I went looking for Lieut. Julius A. Sakus, of Passaic, N. J., long a leader of the battalion's assault platoons. He and his platoon sealed scores of Jap caves on four hills on which the battalion fought.

"It's a swell job," said Lieut. Sakus. "I love the work. Because when you let go with a demolition charge — you know you've got them."

"How does an assault platoon work?"

"It's a simple method. We form a party to clean out enemy pockets, where the troops can't get at the Japs. The Japs dig in, in pill boxes and caves and holes and tunnels.

"The troops have spotted a Jap cave with perhaps 25 Japs in it. The caves support each other with machine gun fire. We of the assault platoon want to get within 15 feet of that cave to let it have a charge. So we draw on friendly troops for support.

"The riflemen get as close as they can, up to 25 or 35 yards from the cave. We move in, crawling, clawing our way up ahead of them. Automatic riflemen are a few feet behind us.

"Now an assault team is made up of two men, one carrying a charge of 30 pounds of TNT; the other a 15-foot bamboo pole. The charge is put on a C ration board rigged to the pole, with a primacord to set off the charge, and dynamite caps to detonate it.

"While we are crawling up to the cave, machine guns and riflemen fire at the cave. Others pick off nearby snipers.

"We get up into position, a few feet from the cave. We lay down and start pushing the charge in. When I start the fuse, we have 15 seconds to get out of there, or be blown up. We have to pull out fast — and we do."

"And what happens after the charge goes off?"

"It seals the cave — we hope. Usually it does. The tunnels cave in, and the entrance is closed forever. Sometimes we see smoke and dirt coming out above the cave. Then we know there is another entrance to seal. We go and get it.

"Sometimes we can hear the Japs dying in the cave, or killing themselves with hand grenades when they know they are sealed in.

"After all, a Jap-held cave is in a stationary position. The Japs can't maneuver. First we get the snipers; then we isolate the cave with machine gun fire, and then we crawl up and seal it with a TNT explosion.

"It's great sport, mister, and there's nothing like it!"

« 18 »

Seven WACS and Seven Joes

SEVEN VETERANS of the Red Arrow Division, soldiers right out of the front lines on the Villa Verde Trail in the Caraballo Mountains, were riding up to the headquarters of the Wacs in a six-ton truck.

The GI's, including three veteran Michigan men, were singing lustily as they rode up to the gate:

"Look out! Look out!

"Here comes the Thirty-second,

"The mighty Thirty-second,

"The fighting Thirty-second,

"Look out! Look out!"

A pretty Wac technical sergeant watched the Red Arrow men jump nimbly out of the truck.

"My gosh," she said, "how did you boys get out of the mountains?"

"Just a bunch of lucky GI's, Sergeant," said Sylvester Krupa, of 4850 Underwood avenue, Detroit. Krupa was six hours out of the front lines. He said he hadn't talked to an American girl since the division left Australia a long, long time ago.

Corp. Ashley Ormsby, who has an Army rating as a second cook's helper but is a very capable public relations officer of the Wacs, was Ashley-on-the-spot.

Very gingerly she introduced the seven front-line soldiers to seven Wacs. Our soldiers were all smiles. The Wacs were very smart looking, in their uniforms—with skirts.

"Now look, boys," said Corp. Ormsby, after the introductions were over, "don't think our Wacs dress this way every day. They haven't been in skirts for a year. They're just wearing skirts, instead of slacks, for this moving picture reel."

"That's fine," said Sergt. Frank J. Tomsej, of 13439 Gallagher avenue, Detroit. "I like our American girls—in skirts."

The soldiers were on a three-day pass to Manila while the Army Pictorial Service shot 3,000 feet of moving picture film on their holiday, mostly about GI's spending a day with the Wacs.

It was, incidentally, a very nice party. The soldiers and the Wacs were very chummy. I went along to watch Corp. Milton Snyder, of Chicago, and Corp. Bob Joeckel, of Pompton Lakes, N. J., veteran cameramen of the Signal Corps, shoot the film.

I admired these two cameramen immensely anyway. They have gone right up into the front lines and shot combat action stuff. They have made many landings with our troops.

Sergt. Viola L. McClean, 5024 Parker avenue, Detroit, a stenographer for the chief quartermaster's division, who has been overseas a year, was paired with Pfc. Krupa of the cavalry reconnaissance troops.

Tech. Sergt. Ivy M. Wing, of 679 Warren avenue west, Detroit, a quartermaster's stenog, and overseas a year, was with Sergt. Tomsej.

Sgt. Mary Katherine Petrides, 207 Hamilton avenue, Flint, also a year overseas, was with Corp. Warren W. Blodgett, 657 Scribner avenue, Grand Rapids.

The Michigan boys told the Michigan girls about their 13-minute broadcast for Radio Station WWJ-The Detroit News, about their 33 days behind the Jap lines wth the cavalry reconnaissance, ambushes, Jap antics, and all.

"My gosh," said Sergt Petrides, "you boys do wonderful things."

"But today, in this movie," laughed Corp. Blodgett, "we're just a bunch of pin-up boys."

There was gay laughter, laughter that was good to hear, boy-meets-girl laughter so rare in the Southwest Pacific.

We started out in the six-ton Army truck. The Wacs and the soldiers visited a beautiful Chinese pagoda, in a picturesque setting, with a pool surrounded by a frog orchestra in giant statuettes, a bull frog with yellow eyes as the impresario.

Before a pool with silvery fish, some of the boys captured a black-and-white goat. A big tom turkey raced by. Cochon pigs squealed under shady trees with fragrant red hibiscus flowers.

The cameramen ground away. Then we went to the market outside the Church of Quiapo, with nine Liberators roaring overhead.

A bar of soap and a pocket comb cost a peso (50 cents) each. House slippers were 14 pesos ($7).

Our party stood in the foyer of the church, watching the Filipino women, very devout, taking off their slippers, and moving slowly down the church aisle toward the altar, 100 yards away, praying on their knees as they went.

Then the GI's took the Wacs to the Panciteria Autogua restaurant for lunch, a meal of Chinese food—chow mein, chop suey, egg fooyung, cheese spread for butter, coffee and orange pop, and bananas and mangoes for dessert.

Sergt. Wing said the Wacs had always wanted to visit the Walled City of Manila, an exotic city of the Orient, centuries old, but now in ruins after the battle there.

With typical GI gallantry, the men of the 32nd got them into the ruins, for fighting men have a way of getting permission to go everywhere but home in the Army.

Everything was in ruins, mere shells of once concrete Spanish-type houses. It seemed sad, all agreed, that the once magnificent Roman Catholic Cathedral of Manila, first built in 1581 and five times destroyed by fire and earthquake, was again in ruins.

After movie shots on the walls, the party left for the Malacanan palace of the Commonwealth, strolling through the spacious shaded, entrancing grounds; paddling on the river in Filipino outrigger canoes, drinking ice cold water in the palace.

It was mess time when we got back to Wac headquarters, and the seven men were guests of the seven Wacs for dinner.

"It's been a wonderful day," said Sergt. McClean.

"The boys are just swell," said Sergt. Wing.

"And," said Sergt. Petrides, "they're taking us to a dance tonight."

The soldiers had little to say. They were in a hurry to get back to the Signal Corps camp to shave, don new sun-tan uniforms and get to the dance.

« 19 »

WACS on the Villa Verde Front

THERE HAS BEEN a lot of good-natured kidding back home on the stage and on the movie screen about the Wac, but the Wacs of USASOS are doing a grand job and a very important one.

There are a thousand Wacs at the USASOS general depot in Manila, which is responsible for the success of movements of supplies to the combat troops, alloting ammunition and food. Some of these Wacs help do "the paper work" which moves supplies six hours away to the 32nd Division fighting on the Villa Verde Trail in the Caraballo Mountains of Northern Luzon.

The Wacs were only five miles from the front when they came into Manila. They took 365 days to leap frog from Brisbane, Australia, up the coast to New Guinea, to Leyte and, finally, to Manila. They fought insects, mud and dust from Hollandia, in New Guinea, to Manila—four thousand miles of personal discomfort to do their jobs without complaint.

These Wacs can take it! They do 75 specialized jobs for the Women's Army Corps, necessary jobs; and 2,500 of them in the Southwest Pacific have relieved that many soldiers for forward duty.

Our girls at war do all manner of things. They convert American money to Australian, Dutch and new Philippine victory money for vast Army payrolls. They are bookkeepers, statisticians, finance clerks. They are hospital technicians and dieticians; they are cryptographers and radio and code clerks for the Signal Corps.

I talked to 17 Michigan Wacs for several hours. Most of them had been overseas for a year; most of them had been in the Wacs for two years or more.

They were typical American girls in uniform, intensely interested in their jobs, amused at the whistles from passing GI's, proud of the Yank fighting men, taking hardships in their stride.

Take Corp. Iola L. Desarmeaux, of Farmington, Mich., who once worked for my old friend Ralph Oyler, chief of the Federal Narcotics Bureau in Detroit and now a stenographer for personnel, for instance.

Corp. Desarmeaux got through an hour and a half air raid in Leyte, with the Jap bombs dropping, and her only reaction was that she was able to make up work the same day.

Sergt. Lucille E. Turnquist, of Grand Rapids, a statistician for the quartermaster, was one of five Wacs who were the first white women to reach Maruko, in Dutch New Guinea.

"Our boys hadn't seen an American girl for a long time," she said. "About 100 of them stood around, very enthusiastic as they told us about their new equipment. They were swell boys."

Sergt. Suzanne F. Leland, of Saugatuck, Mich., a medical technician, made her first airplane trip, and it was an eight-hour ride from Hollandia to Tacloban in Leyte.

"Inflation sure has hit Manila," she said. "A nickel bar of soap costs two pesos ($1), cantaloupe a la mode is four pesos ($2), in one place a $4 pair of shoes cost 85 pesos (about $43)."

Corp. Grace S. Ross, of Dearborn, who once worked for the Veterans Hospital there, works in the headquarters payroll section.

When I saw Capt. Evangeline L. Kohel, of Grand Rapids, she was busy checking and rechecking a bookkeeping "shortage" of 79 pesos, 40 centavos, in a payroll of 10,500 pesos.

"I will find the darn thing if it takes all night," she said.

Corp. Beatrice E. Low, 13129 Cherrylawn avenue, Detroit, thought a Jap air raid at Tacloban, Leyte, was "more exciting than scaring."

Sergt. Marjorie M. Woida, RFD 5, Pontiac, who works in the Wac dispensary, said she "hoped to get to Tokyo with our troops, but Uncle Sam will decide if I do."

Corp. Grace S. Sanford, of Milan, Mich., a file clerk for the message center, said she "liked the climate of New Guinea better than Manila."

In a convoy from Hollandia to Manila, Sergt. Mary Josefowich, Flint, watched the protecting Navy ships "shoot up two Jap mines in two days."

"Seeing Manila, a city bombed and destroyed, is being close to war and I wouldn't trade the experience for anything," said Sergt. Martha G. Van Gansbeke, of Mulliken, Mich.

Meeting a "couple of boys from home" in New Guinea from the 32nd Division was immensely enjoyed by Pfc. Muriel Larson, of Calumet.

Sergt. Rachel C. Richards, of Muskegon, had a harrowing experience with 68 other Wacs on a Dutch tug taking them from Brisbane to Hollandia.

"The trip took 12 days and it was rough," she said. "There were sheep and chickens at one end of the tug, and we were at the other end. We watched some Indian cooks put a big steak on the dirty mess floor and chop it up with an ax. That was too much for us. We had five Wac cooks with us and they cooked mess from then on."

Sergt. Lucille Hembree, 25815 Van Born avenue, Dearborn, transportation file clerk, met her brother at Hollandia, Seaman John R. Hembree, for the first time in almost two years.

As I talked with her, Sergt. Hembree was with Pfc. Robert L. Spicer, of 1435 Seventeenth street, Dearborn, an infantry rifleman. They once lived in the same block back home.

"I've been standing guard nights, and Sergt. Hembree has been working three nights a week, so we haven't had much opportunity to talk," Spicer said.

Sergt. Emeline J. McCowen, of 116 West street, Battle Creek, a cryptographer, spent two weeks on a refrigerator ship with many stormy days, to get to Manila. "I was the first one to get seasick," she laughed.

Seeing Manila, "something I had always read about and seeing bananas as they grow was something," said Pvt. Irene T. Fredryk, of Hamtramck, a Signal Corps service clerk.

Sergt. Alma Eve Davies, of Grand Rapids, a medical technician, had a friendly pup with her that adopted her in Leyte.

"I was in Manila eight years ago when it was one of the most beautiful cities in the world," she said. "It made me just sick to see it destroyed by war."

I caught a view of Pfc. Dorothy Lagace, who was born in Schaeffer, Mich., a Wac mail clerk, handing out mail to a group of Wacs as hungry for "sugar dispatches" from home as the GI's.

« 20 »

Nothing Stops the GI Road Gangs

THE RAINY SEASON began in the Philippines with tropical downpours cascading torrents of water on the Villa Verde Trail and knocking out the retaining walls, in some places, on the mountain road the Engineers had labored so hard to build.

I saw Staff Sergt. Frank T. Taylor, of 1522 Montclair avenue, Detroit, the day after his promotion in the 114th Engineer Combat Battalion. He had just rushed 10,000 sandbags up the Villa Verde Trail while a group of Michigan boys backtracked over the trail, doing their work all over again as they filled in washed out retaining walls with sandbags.

"We've hauled 700,000 sandbags up the Villa Verde since we began building the road," Sergt Taylor said. "You can say it again, those are a lot of sandbags. But it takes 40,000 sandbags just for an artillery emplacement."

For 105 days the Engineers have been working on the Villa Verde and Sergt. Taylor said, with pride ringing in his voice, that "the Engineers sure have done a magnificent job up there." Everyone in the division has conceded that.

We chatted about some Michigan men who were up front on the trail, widening the road, using power saw drills on the outside bank, and blowing out large boulders with six to eight-pound charges of TNT. And all this under constant Jap sniper fire and occasional Jap artillery and mortar fire.

There is nothing braver in the 6th Army than an Engineer road construction gang, laboring alternately in the broiling sun and then in the thunderstorms of the rainy season and then in the sun again, always in danger, constantly under fire.

Some of the Michigan men working on the eight-foot road on the Villa-Verde, as we talked, included:

Sergt. Bert H. Corsette, 2106 Portage avenue, Kalamazoo; Sergt. John V. Bukala, 344 Houseman avenue northeast, Grand Rapids; Sergt. Earl L. Newton, 1152 Huizenga avenue, Muskegon Heights; Corp. Ernest L. Bernard, Garden City; and Pfc. Leonard W. Bassett, 700 State street, Bay City.

While we were talking I watched Corp. John Morse, 4266 Maybury Grand avenue, Detroit, who has been overseas 37 months, repairing a five-foot cross-cut saw with a file. The boys call him "Pop," and he is the sharpener for all axes and saws used on the Villa Verde.

"Our boys are proud of the job they are doing," Sergt. Taylor remarked. "They use coils of Manila rope, hitching the rope to tree trunks and rocks so they can scramble up the steep mountainside to place their demolition charges.

"Why, only this week I sent up 200 shovels and picks for Filipino laborers working on washed out retaining walls, so we can put sandbag fills in."

The armored bulldozer which the GI's call The Cat and The Dozer, is now working 100 to 200 yards ahead of the infantry.

The dozer driver has only two small slits to look through.

Two non-coms follow it, and another acts as a guide on the hillside, all staying under cover. They throw rocks on the right side of the bulldozer cab or the left to warn the driver to swing a little right or left.

"One dozer driver, a soldier named Arkie," said Sergt. Taylor, "cut a swathe out of a mountainside, and sealed up three Japs in a cave. He didn't see them. A lieutenant rushed up and pounded on his cab. 'Hey, Arkie,' he said, 'You've knocked off three Nips.'

"Well, Arkie got out of his cab, and some riflemen rushed up with a Jap flag and a Jap officer's saber.

" 'We want you to have this, Arkie,' they said. 'You saved us a lot of trouble sealing up those Nips.' "

Only yesterday one bulldozer driver spotted a Jap machine gun nest on the trail. He went in after them with his "cat." They plastered the armored cab with machine gun bullets. Bullets cut the cable on the bulldozer blade and made it useless.

"So this engineer crawled out of his cab," Sergt. Taylor said, "and shouted at the Nips, 'You blankety-blank ——!' and then he ducked. A ricocheting bullet nipped him across the forehead, but it was only a superficial wound. What a guy!"

Two bulldozer drivers were buried in landslides. Their Engineer-pals dug them out. They spent a week in the hospital, and then came back to their construction work.

It was Sunday, as we talked, so the Detroit boys invited me over to the Engineers mess for a chicken dinner. I met Pfc. Daniel J. Frederick, 263 Colonial avenue south, Detroit, a cook who had helped prepare the meal.

Someone put down a big plate of chicken in front of me and Pfc. William E. Lanzen, who used to work at 147 Lake Shore drive, Grosse Pointe Farms, said, "How are things back home?"

He laughed, a full throated laugh, when your war correspondent remarked that "the folks back home don't have any better Sunday dinners than this one, pal."

« 21 »

"Brooklyn" Wins a Stripe

YOU MAY HAVE wondered how an untried, green soldier feels when he shows the stuff of which heroes are made.

Well, 19-year-old John F. Cerese, of Brooklyn, a rifleman for Company B, 128th Infantry, won a battlefield promotion from private first class to sergeant, and a Silver Star, all in his first five days of combat.

"And I was scared pink," said Cerese.

The new sergeant was unashamed as he made the confession. He had crawled 60 feet under enemy fire to within 20 feet of the Jap positions and carried out a wounded comrade under fire. Then he crawled up to a cave, where four Nips were hiding, pushed in a demolition charge and threw seven hand grenades. He killed all the Japs.

But he was scared. It was nothing new. For all good fighting men at one time or another get that creepy feeling they are never going to get back home.

I have met many brave fighting men at the front, whose courage has been tried and tested many times under fire, and none of them has ever been ashamed to admit that all brave men know fear and conquer it nonetheless.

I can't forget what this young Brooklyn soldier's regimental commander told him as he promoted him to sergeant, jumping Cerese right over veteran corporals.

Col. Merle H. Howe, of 621 Deming street east, Grand Rapids, Mich., his commander, is a terrific fighting man and a great leader of troops himself. Col. Howe won the Silver Star at Buna for gallantry in action, the Distinguished Service Cross, also at Buna, for conspicuous gallantry, the Bronze

Star for meritorious service at Aitape. He won the Purple Heart at Buna and the oak leaf cluster on the Villa Verde.

Col. Howe was 40 feet away as Sergt. Cerese brought the wounded soldier in, and 10 feet away as Cerese blew up the Japs. Regimental commanders on the Villa Verde are always in the front lines with their men.

"I liked the way you came up on that Jap cave," Col. Howe told him. "You showed you had the guts to go in there and you showed you knew how to make the approach. That's why we're making you a sergeant and a squad leader. I think you know how to lead men."

Later, Sergt. Cerese said, "You'd go to hell and back for a commander like him. All the boys like him."

Sergt. Cerese has been in the Army 10 months. He came overseas only two months ago. Two days after he got into the line he killed a Jap with his Garand at 30 feet.

He was the first scout with a six-man demolition squad. His sergeant told him to bypass two caves. On the squad's return, the Japs opened up on the squad from 20-foot range, wounding the sergeant, who was able to get back to his lines, and seriously wounding a soldier with a pole charge of TNT.

Col. Howe was standing out in the open when the squad came in.

"We ought to get that wounded man out of there," he said.

"I felt a little shaky about going back," said Sergt. Cerese, "but it was one of our boys out there. So another fellow and I started crawling out. We had to go 60 feet to get him. The Japs banged away at us—but missed.

"I had to prop the wounded soldier up. He was hit in the stomach. The Japs were firing. We didn't dare lift him up. He might have been hit again. So we dragged him out, slowly, so as not to hurt him more. He never complained, he was a brave guy."

When they got the wounded man in and Col. Howe had

come up closer to help them, the colonel said, "That's a good job, men. Now we'll have to blow up those caves."

Sergt. Cerese and his companion got a demolition pole charge and started after the Nips. Col. Howe and Col. Ernest A. Barlow, of Salt Lake City, the chief of staff, followed close behind the two enlisted men.

After the charge had been detonated and the grenades thrown, Col. Howe leaned over the cave and stuck his head in to make sure the Japs were dead.

"I wouldn't have stuck my head in that cave for all of Henry Ford's dough," said Cerese.

The Japs fired knee mortars at the Yanks before the cave. They dropped to the ground. Cerese's companion was wounded by a mortar shell fragment. Col. Barlow was hit in the finger, but stayed at the front.

Col. Howe was struck in the leg. He refused to leave the front lines. He was limping up there two days later, still with his men.

"When you're led by officers like that," said Sergt. Cerese, "well, hell, guys like me can do about anything, I guess."

« 22 »

Engineers Work Miracles

THE ENGINEERS HAD a tough time for 107 days building more than 20 miles of the Little Burma Road over the footpath Villa Verde Trail, but now that the rainy season has started the Engineers are working harder than ever to keep the road in.

The road must stay in, despite landslides, cave-ins, and water that washes revetments away. The Little Burma must stay, since over it flow all the vital supplies that keep the Red Arrow Division fighting.

Capt. Philip Cantor, of New York, head of the reconnaissance troops for the 114th Combat Engineers, had a typical experience on the Little Burma. He was driving over the road in his jeep. A mountain landslide came rolling down with an uprooted tree hurtling through it. He smashed on his brakes, put his car in reverse, and almost backed into a second one. He found himself marooned between two landslides. But he got his jeep out, finally.

"In 15 minutes," Capt. Cantor said, "the Engineers had the road repaired!"

The Little Burma is one of the finest feats of engineering anywhere. It cuts around and around the mountains like a giant hairpin and it has perhaps more hairpin turns than any other road in the world!

The Little Burma rises 22 feet vertical for every 100 feet of horizontal roadway, so that Army vehicles can make the grades. One of the most amazing things about its construction is that only 550 engineers built it, working 12 hours a day with an armored bulldozer in front of the infantry, six other dozers, two graders and 15 dump trucks.

The road has held up surprisingly well through the heavy torrents of the rainy season, which act as if somebody had opened a giant porthole and let the whole Pacific Ocean in.

But water rolls down the cliffs from 500 feet above the road and washes out the revetment-wall. Engineers build up the sides with sandbags. They dig down 10 feet and make an underground log stockade to fill up the washed out wall. Otherwise vehicles would go over the sides. Patrols of 10 engineers go out looking for breaks in the road like this, climb down the mountainside, cut down trees with hacksaws in the draws far below, haul the trees up for the stockades.

The artillery has its own bulldozers. So the artillery bulldozers have been assigned sections of the road. When the rain washes out a side of the road, these bulldozers go to work like firemen on a five-alarm fire.

It always interested me to know how this road was built, a road eight feet wide and as wide as 20 feet on some steep turns, over a foot-and-a-half trail.

"First I took out recon patrols," Capt. Cantor said. "We stayed out from two to 12 days, out in front of the infantry, trying to avoid combat, fighting it out when necessary. We made sketches of the existing trail, studied the type of ground it was, whether the mountains could be cut away and still support vehicles, what construction obstacles would be encountered on the way.

"On these recon trips, sometimes 10 miles ahead of the troops, we decided what road building equipment we needed and if we didn't have it we borrowed it.

"We started out using unarmed bulldozers. The Nips picked off some of our drivers and suicidal Jap infiltration parties tried to wipe out the dozers. So we borrowed an armed cab, put three guides near the driver—because he makes so much noise he can't hear a thing—and a 12-man guard of engineers to protect the dozer from the enemy.

"The artillery and machine guns of the enemy have been directed at the dozers, but they have kept on working. One day a dozer was working on the road, its reverse gear stuck. It went over the side, with its big blade keeping it upright. The driver jumped out. With his rifle in his hands he followed the dozer down 700 feet. As it hit a valley, he jumped in and got it under control. Then it took him eight hours to build a road back up with his blade!

"The dozers hack away at the mountainside, and push the dirt over the side down 300 to 1,500-foot drops. Once an armored cab got in some loose dirt on the cliff, and went over.

"In the rain it is hard work building the road—and we are

still pushing ahead. We built only 50 yards of road today. The mud was four feet deep. Engineers had to use hand shovels so the dozers could work along. The mud was so deep the dozers couldn't get traction. The dozers do the rough work and the graders cut it down and smooth out the road.

"Only the other day at our headquarters in the foothills a group of engineers got in a four-hour fight with some infiltrating Japs. They killed nine. At night, up on the trail, the engineers at work on the roads form their own perimeter defenses."

Capt. Cantor suddenly thought of something, chuckling to himself.

"Our engineers on the trail always have hot food," he said. "You just can't beat the GI's for ingenious ways of making their own comfort.

"Our road builders take cans of C rations about 10:30 a. m. every morning and set them next to the exhaust pipes on the dozers, or hang them over the exhaust pipes of trucks. At noon they have a nice hot meal ready and waiting."

« 23 »

In and Out of a Jap Ambush

THE NIPS TRIED to ambush three Michigan soldiers up on a mountain peak a mile high, but the Michigan GI's shot their way out and killed three Japs.

It was a sharp, fast fight at close range, but our boys won it. They had just received their orders to go back home on rotation. They were starting down a mountain trail, on their way to the rear, where they could start by jeep for a ship to take them home.

"No blankety-blank Nip was going to stop us," said Sergt. Lloyd Robert Wiser, 510 Douglas street north, Bronson, Mich.

Pfc. Robert E. Mugride, 340 Capitol avenue southwest, Battle Creek, Pfc. Herbert J. Taylor, 130 Garfield avenue west, Coldwater, and Wiser fought their way down the trail. The three were all in their fourth year of service overseas with the division's 126th Infantry.

Pfc. Mugride said he was "just lucky to be able to go home." The day before his rotation orders arrived a Jap sniper's bullet passed through his helmet without hitting him!

"Just a lucky stiff is Muggy," he said.

Two rifle companies fought their way to some hard-won positions on a Jap-held hill overlooking the "Little Burma Road."

That night the Japs launched two fanatical Banzai attacks on their positions, trying to push the Yanks down the slope into the draw where Jap machine guns could slaughter them where they would have no cover.

But the Yanks didn't push!

Maj.-Gen. William H. Gill, division commander, and Col. Frederick R. Stofft, commander of the 127th Infantry Regiment, personally commended Pfc. Victor Ostrowski, 9722 Yellowstone street, Detroit.

The Detroit machine gunner, with three other members of his gun section, placed his heavy machine gun on the flanks of the two rifle companies. There was a full moon when the Nips attacked in force.

Ostrowski held his fire until the Japs were close. Then, with a perfect concentration of fire, Ostrowski's machine gun section smashed one Jap counterattack, got ready for the second and smashed it.

"It was an excellent supporting action," said Col. Stofft.

Ostrowski is a fine fighting man, veteran of sharp clashes on both Leyte and Luzon, and winner of the Purple Heart, the Philippine Liberation Medal and the Combat Infantryman's Badge.

"The action was a little hot that night," Ostrowski said. "But we picked out a very nice spot and it was like shooting ducks in a barrel when the Nips came up screaming. We gave 'em something to scream about."

All the really remarkable work that is being done in this divison is not done by the fighting troops themselves. I don't want to depreciate what they do, but there are others in the division who do important, necessary jobs.

Consider the work of Corp. John Heldo, Jr., 139 Forman avenue north, Detroit, and Pfc. Joseph G. Correa, 1020 Vernor Highway west, Detroit.

It is their job to assist in maintaining the smooth flow of supplies up the "Little Burma Road" to the frontline troops of the 127th Infantry.

No job is more important. The troops can't fight without their supplies of ammo, food, water, sandbags, drugs and bandages. Those supplies must come up and they must come up on schedule.

And the supplies have moved without hit-or-miss, come

heavy rains, Jap snipers and mortars and landslides on Villa Verde. Supplymen like Heldo and Correa work 10 and 12 hours a day getting the supplies up forward.

They have supervised Filipino ration trains up the trail, under cover of darkness, when the mortars and the sniping were too hot to use trucks.

"Our ration parties have had some close calls," Correa said, "but we always keep on going!"

The Filipinos are grateful to the Yank troops who are driving the Japs out of northern Luzon, so that peace can once more come to the Philippines.

Filipinos shout, "Hello, Joe!" and "Mabuhay, Joe," and some of the shy Filipino women say "Mahal kita, Joe." Mabuhay means "A long life!" and "Mahal kita" means "You are very dear to us."

So the Commonwealth of the Philippines has responded by awarding the prized Philippine Liberation Medal to Yank soldiers who have fought in Luzon and Leyte. To get the medal, a soldier in the 32nd has to be recommended by Gen. Gill.

Some of the Detroiters who received the Liberation Medal include Corp. Harold A. Beauregard, 3741 Bishop road; Pfc. Royal Mull, 13431 Lumpkin street; Sergt. Robert T. Morris, 9449 Henely Place, who was just promoted from private first class.

Pfc. Louis Rosebaum, 2951 Webb avenue; Corp. James E. Morton, 65 Ford avenue, Highland Park; Pfc. William G. Anderson, 14865 Mendota avenue; Pfc. Ted J. Cronander, 5903 Belvidere avenue; Corp. Lew W. Watterson, 1620 Forest avenue west.

Sergt. Joseph G. Leitheim, 4946 Lawndale avenue; Pvt. Harold J. Bradley, 5966 Sixteenth street.

Sergt. Chester J. Wrukowski, 3488 Burns avenue, was awarded the Combat Infantryman's Badge for "exemplary conduct under enemy fire."

« 24 »

Medics Are Heroic Too

THE MEDICAL AID men, the litter bearers and the ambulance drivers are close to every infantryman's heart.

A rifleman brought in under fire, bandaged under fire, his life saved with a tourniquet, never forgets. Nor do his pals who trained with him in the United States and fought through six campaigns overseas with him, ever forget!

The life of a medical aid man and a litter bearer at the front in the Caraballo Mountains is a precarious one. So you may have an idea what these men of mercy go through, I talked for a long time with eight of them from Michigan.

We were sitting on cots in a squad tent—Corp. Harold A. Beauregard, 3471 Bishop road, Detroit, a litter bearer; Sergt. Joseph J. Thompson, 1127 Front street, Grand Rapids, a supply man for medics at the front; Pfc. George B. Gielawa, 915 Park avenue southwest, Grand Rapids, a litter bearer.

Also with us were Corp. Gideon E. Millar, 12245 Hamilton avenue, Highland Park, an ambulance driver; Corp. Roger L. Santure, 302 Fourth street east, Monroe, a truck driver for supplies; Corp. Vincent L. Schmitz, an ambulance driver from Chelsea; Sergt. Joseph A. Turowski, 8551 Kenney street, Detroit, the litter bearers' mess sergeant.

Sergt. Claude B. Van Wormer, 202 Madison avenue, Flint, is the noncom in charge of a company of litter bearers and ambulance drivers.

In your war correspondent's notebook some of the conversation on how the wounded are gotten out of the mountains was taken down as follows:

Beauregard: "It took us two and one-half hours to get one

wounded soldier to the battalion aid station from the line, the trail was so slippery. Four of us were wrestling with his litter. We got him in and he said, 'Thanks, pals.'"

Millar: "It took our litter team four hours to bring one rifleman in. It would have taken 25 minutes to walk in by yourself. But the thick brush and the steep mountain slope made it tough to get him in."

Thompson: "We got pinned down by Jap knee mortars. They spotted us and tried to wipe us out. What a bunch of _____'s!"

Gielawa: "We made a 'daisy chain' of litter bearers so we could keep passing litters with wounded up the slope. Isn't that right, Oscar?"

Schmitz: "That was it. It was a hot spot from enemy fire."

Beauregard: "Sometimes the Japs let you get through to the wounded. As you start out with your litter their snipers open up and pin you down. Infantry patrols come out to give us cover."

Gielawa: "It rained four times one day. I was riding in the back of an ambulance with the wounded. Kept the back door open for emergency. We started to slide over a cliff. I pulled the men out, and put them on the trail. It was enough to scare hell out of you."

Santure: "The rainy season has been tough. We put a three-quarter ton in front of an ambulance and another three-quarter behind it. Then we chained them all together so they could get down the Villa Verde, at night with no lights, with the wounded."

Millar: "On those wild rides down the Villa Verde I always sit back with the patients and reassure them. They look out and see those big drops down the cliff. They can't wait till we get them in."

They explained there are two medical aid men with a rifle platoon. They bandage the wounded, give them shots of morphine and call for the litter bearers. These wait at the advance command posts in litter squads of four men to a litter.

Beauregard: "It took 12 of us to get one man over the trail."

Van Wormer: "Once we used 16 Filipinos from the battalion aid station to the collecting point. That was for speed and it still took us three hours."

Schmitz: "We get 'em on the litters fast. Our record is still 45 seconds from the time a soldier was hit until we had him."

Turowski: "It's hot up there. We lost eight killed and nine wounded among our litter bearers."

Beauregard: "The 1st Battalion had three killed and seven wounded in two days. One ambulance was hit; an orderly, a Detroit litter bearer and the ambulance driver were all wounded."

Millar: "A litter squad makes about three hauls a day. At night we stay with the perimeter defense of whatever infantry company we're with.

"When there's a night attack, the medical aid man asks for volunteers from among the litter bearers. It is rough moving around at night because our riflemen stay in their positions and bang away at any thing that moves ahead of them."

Corp. Ross J. Baker, of 8785 Quincy avenue, Detroit, a driver, walked up and stood there listening.

"Those night litter bearers who volunteer for that work have the stuff," he said.

They all have it in the 107th Medical Battalion!

« 25 »

A Note to Those Who Wait

OF COURSE you worry back home.

You worry about the chap you know as a sweetheart, or as a brother, son or a father—the chap who was one of America's best in civilian life and who is now fighting on the "Little Burma Road" with the Red Arrow Division against frenzied Jap opposition.

I sometimes think that those who sit and wait back home, with the threat of a telegram from the War Department hanging over them, possess a noble courage, too.

Of course you wonder what chance your man has when he's hit, by a Jap sniper, by Jap machine guns, by mortar and artillery shrapnel, what chance he has of coming back to you.

Up here in the mountains—the most difficult terrain in the world to get wounded out—96 per cent of all the 32nd's wounded are saved!

Ninety-six out of every 100 wounded soldiers are saved by medical courage and medical skill, on the battlefield and behind the lines, by medics whom the fighting men love like brothers because of their work.

There isn't an infantryman in the line, if you ask him a question about what unit is tops in the division, who won't reply without hesitation, "The medics, by God!"

I have seen in the field the splendid work that the 107th Medical Battalion of the Red Arrow Division is doing. I have spent days sitting around talking to its personnel, for what the medics do gives you a feeling of assurance at the front.

Lieut.-Col. Herbert C. Wallace, of 118 Oakley street south, Saginaw, is the commander of the 107th Medical Battalion. It operates three portable hospitals, a clearing station in the foothills, nine collecting companies and nine clearing companies.

The battalion has 12 top-notch medical officers, surgeons and experienced doctors; 13 medical administration officers who keep 407 enlisted men—medical aids, litter bearers, ambulance drivers, medical technicians—at work with the esprit de corps of a championship team that never watches the clock.

Medic aids dress wounds on the battlefield. Litter bearers carry the wounded to battalion aid stations at the front, stations where plasma is given and wounds are re-dressed. The portable hospitals are along the Villa Verde Trail and wounded are rushed there in ambulances to get immediate treatment, sometimes operations an hour after they are hit that save their lives.

The big clearing station in the foothills, 15 miles from the front, is equipped to take care of 200 patients.

On some days it has evacuated 100 patients by Piper Cubs, many of them furnished to the division by the pennies collected by patriotic school children of Detroit. They are moved to two field hospitals far to the rear, field hospitals that have all the modern, fine equipment of the hospitals you know back home.

All this is done under enemy fire at the front, under harassing sniper fire down the trail. The hospitals near the front are constantly vigilant for Jap infiltration parties.

This clearing station run by Col. Wallace has an ice cream making machine. It also has a "reefer," a refrigerator on wheels, which provides the wounded with ice cold water, far different from the tepid canteen-water they knew at the front.

The station has its own surgery with wards in tents and enlisted men trained as nurses. Sergt. Paul E. Normandin, 485 Bennett street west, Detroit, is a surgical technician, who assisted in 471 operations last month.

"I guess I'll go to medical college when I get back to Detroit," he said.

The station has the only dental laboratory in the Southwest Pacific that is operated for its own division alone. I saw Pfc. David W. Cohen, 2529 Elmhurst avenue, Detroit, mixing fillings. I watched a Wisconsin technician grinding out 100 plates on a machine for false teeth for front-line troops.

Col. Wallace told me that originally this was almost completely a Michigan outfit. One collecting company and one ambulance company came from Bay City, one clearing company from Belding, a collecting company from Monroe and a clearing company and a headquarters company from Detroit.

"All our Michigan boys have been doing a great job for the wounded," he said.

They sure have.

« 26 »

Medics Never Rest

THE MEDICS are always under fire. They are not fighting men and under the rules of the Geneva Convention they are supposed to work among the wounded without being fired upon by civilized soldiers at war. But the Jap breaks all the rules concerning the medics.

Those attached to Lieut.-Col. Herbert C. Wallace's 107th Medical Battalion are not soldiers, but they have and will fight for their patients.

I was sitting in an administrative tent with Col. Wallace when he turned to First Lieut. Benjamin A. Mayer of Milwaukee, Wis.

"Ben," he said, "tell him about Sergt. Richardson, of Bay City, will you? It's a great story."

I turned my head. I was watching another Michigan man at work around me at the medical headquarters, Sergt. George T. Tulauskas, Ferndale, a platoon sergeant for surgery. I heard a headquarters noncom shout, "Hey, Curly," at Staff Sergt. Harold W. Calhoun, 2596 Bewick avenue, Detroit.

Lieut. Mayer said he thought what Sergt. Richardson had done was typical of the way the medics will fight—only when they have to—for the wounded Yanks entrusted to their care.

They called Sergt. Albert M. Richardson, Bay City, "Buck." Buck Richardson had been awarded the Silver Star by Maj.-Gen. William H. Gill, commander of the division.

"I'll never forget what Buck did," said Col. Wallace, quietly, "when 12 Japs with machine guns, hand grenades and rifles tried to wipe out 50 wounded Yanks.

"He was a sweetheart, that Buck," said Lieut. Mayer.

It happened during the Leyte campaign, before the division came to Northern Luzon. Sergt. Richardson was in charge of a section at a collecting station.

The Japs sneaked in. They ambushed the collecting station, and started to throw a concentration of fire into it. Their firing was high at first, bullets chipping holes in the tops of ward tents.

Now Buck Richardson was in charge of medical aid men, litter bearers and ambulance drivers. He was not a fighting man.

"But Buck had to fight then and there," said Lieut. Mayer. "It was either fight or watch the wounded die. Now who is going to do that? Well, Buck didn't stand by and let that happen."

So Buck Richardson grabbed an infantryman's carbine. Pfc. Don Pickens, a medical technician from Solomonville, Ariz., grabbed another.

They crawled out, just the two of them, toward the Jap positions. They started returning the Jap fire. They killed eight

Japs by rifle fire. Four other Nips started to run. Buck Richardson and Pfc. Pickens shot down three more. Only one got away. Pickens got the Bronze Star.

"They saved all the patients," said Col. Wallace. "Buck said he just got mad and that's the reason he could shoot so straight."

But the Japs were out for revenge. They pulled a heavy mountain gun up from somewhere. They fired registering shots, one over and one short, and then bracketed into the hospital. There were many wounded there. Only one patient was hit. But the 107th Battalion lost four killed and 12 wounded as its personnel labored under fire to get the wounded out.

In an hour, under fire, the medics evacuated 100 patients to the rear and safety. Col. Wallace was standing in the open, supervising the evacuation. One of his men was hit and went down. Col. Wallace carried him in for treatment.

The last truck was ready to go out. Col. Wallace packed it with his men. He stayed behind with five enlisted men, waiting for the truck to come back. The wounded were safe then, but these six waited in their foxholes. Shells were dropping all around them.

The truck finally returned. A shell landed and blew several medics off the truck. Col. Wallace and his group loaded them back on—and away went the truck, running the last gauntlet of shell fire.

"That waiting for the truck to come was the hardest part of it," Col. Wallace said. "We had to sweat it out!"

They showed me a division citation for an enlisted man, a citation posted on the bulletin board. Not many nights ago, he was riding with some wounded Yanks in an ambulance feeling its way down the Little Burma Road.

Two wheels of the ambulance went over the edge of a cliff. The ambulance came down on its ambulance block. That saved it. The driver set the emergency brakes. The orderly got the patients out. He ran down the road for a mile and got an Engineer's bulldozer.

The Engineers pulled the ambulance back on the road. Then the orderly carried the patients back into the ambulance, and away it went to the portable hospital.

It is this devotion to the wounded that has made the 107th Battalion so popular in the Red Arrow Division.

These medics are a great bunch of guys!

« 27 »

Red Blood Saves Lives

WHEN YOU FIRST HEAR about medical supply, it doesn't sound very glamorous. It doesn't seem at first hand to have the thrill and the excitement like listening to a GI who has crawled up to a cave housing 25 Japs and blown them to their Shinto gods with a demolition charge of TNT.

Yet there is something magnificent about the officers and enlisted men in medical supply, with the 107th Medical Battalion. The more you hear about them, the more interesting, the more important their job becomes.

Take one item alone, important in the saving of hundreds of infantrymen's lives—real human blood! The medics will tell you it is more effective than blood plasma.

When a wounded soldier suffers from loss of blood, when his veins begin to collapse, only real, live blood will save him. And it is medical supply, unsung, unheralded in the communiques, but respected by all fighting men, that gets this human blood to the portable hospitals, the collecting stations, and the clearing stations where it is needed every day.

Capt. Paul R. Benjamin, of Wellsboro, Pa., is head of medical supply for this division. He is one of those night-and-day administrators, one of those tireless fellows, who knows the quantity of medical supplies a fighting infantry division requires.

It is refreshing to talk with him. He is, incidentally, doing one of the finest jobs in the division, getting medical supplies up front by truck, by carriers, sometimes by those super Piper Cubs, that the school children of Detroit provided with their pennies.

Consider again this important matter of real blood for the wounded. From Jan. 1 to March 31, 1945, the division has used 420 pints of it.

Capt. Benjamin told me all about it. The real blood comes in pint jars, donated by Americans on the West Coast. It comes in a plywood box, 16 glass jars of blood in pints. Inside is a cylindrical metal container which holds the life-saving blood tightly in place. Inside the cylinder is another cylinder that holds ice.

The blood is flown from San Francisco to Oahu, re-iced, and then flown to the New Guinea blood bank; re-iced, and flown to the 32nd Division.

Here it is immediately placed in "the reefer," a portable refrigerator on wheels, and kept at a temperature of 40 degrees. It must be used in nine or ten days—and all of it is.

The "keeper of the reefer," which is run by its own motor, is Corp. Milfred R. Beliveau, 640 Vernor highway west, whom I saw working on the reefer motor, his shirt and undershirt off in the hot sun, his hands and face thick with grease.

"This reefer," he said, "must always work!"

Around him in administrative tents I saw a number of Michigan boys at work, some in the medical supply, others in other units of the 107th.

I saw Staff Sergt. Ralph W. Armstrong, 5229 Campbell avenue, Detroit, of medical supply; Staff Sergt. Harold W.

(Curly) Calhoun, 2596 Bewick avenue, Detroit, at headquarters; Sergt. Forrest E. Sarkella, 309 Avalon, Highland Park, who keeps 100 vehicles running for the medical battalion; Corp. Edwin A. Anderson, 1935 Cortland avenue, Detroit, a mechanic.

All of these boys were sweating it out in the broiling sun in their specialized jobs. Others were Sergt. Henry F. Domanowski, 3880 Yemans avenue, Hamtramck, of the medic communications section; Pfc. Walter L. Froman, 1722 Francis avenue southeast, Grand Rapids, who keeps the parts rolling for the trucks that take up the supplies.

I talked to Warrant Officer Robert M. Bennett, of Midland, Mich., in the headquarters personnel section; Sergt.-Maj. Anthony Piskorski, 2311 Danforth avenue, Hamtramck, the "big boss" of the battalion's enlisted men and non-coms.

And Sergt. Russell R. Zielesch, 1280 Chalmers avenue, Detroit, in personnel, and Staff Sergt. Robert M. Lovell, of Leonard, Mich., who is in the communications section.

All these men work hard, and the jobs they do all co-ordinate into the vast teamplay of the 107th Medical Battalion, the great life-savers of the division.

A division requires a tremendous amount of medical supplies in an action like that taking place in the Caraballo Mountains. Capt. Benjamin dug up the medical statistics for me for three months in the campaign on Luzon and the Villa Verde.

Here they are:

Six hundred and seventy-one litters, 1,349 blankets, 11 medical chests, 15,658 cans of foot powder, 650 units of blood plasma, 788 bottles of dextrose.

Eight hundred and seventy-one dozens of two-inch bandages, 649 dozens of three-inch bandages, 218,000 aspirin tablets, 1,300 vials of penicillin, 370,000 sulfa tablets, 3,019 spools of 1

—2-inch adhesive tape, 1,737 spools of three-inch adhesive, 981 packages of sulfanilamide crystals.

One thousand six hundred and twenty-nine large absorbent dressings, 2,248 small absorbent dressings, 215 pints of paregoric, 12 gallons of merthiolate solution for wounds before an operation, 362 gallons of ethyl alcohol for sterilization, 92 vials of tetanus antitoxin, 233 vials of gas gangrene prophylaxis, 941 vials of tetanus vaccine, 51 of cholera vaccine, 227 of smallpox vaccine and 80 tanks of oxygen in two months.

Is it any wonder that Capt. Benjamin's medical supply section is always busy!

« 28 »

School Children Buy Mercy Planes

THE WOUNDED GI's, two of them with head wounds from Jap shell fragments, were lying on cots under canvas in the American Red Cross tent, waiting.

They said nothing. They had that pinched, drawn look of seriously wounded men. They had been wounded in the hard fighting 6,000 feet up in the Caraballo Mountains. But they did not complain.

A big medical technician from Arkansas leaned over a wounded Yank from Wisconsin, and said, "How are you doing, pal? Want anything?"

"I'm all right, fellows," the wounded man said. The words came out of him slowly, as if they came hard.

"Take it easy," the medic said, "you'll be in a hospital bed in 15 minutes in the finest hospital in the world."

"That's a good deal," the wounded rifleman said, "and— thanks."

"Aw, hell," said the lanky medic from Arkansas in a slow drawl. And then he muttered to himself, "Nothing is too good for you guys."

But he said it to himself, almost inaudibly. He knew wounded soldiers. They hate to have a fuss made over them.

Then in came the Wings of Mercy. Oh, she flew in prettily, banking across a mountain range, as if her right wing would knock off a peak, and sweeping down in a graceful turn, right smack on the little airstrip that only a few months ago had been a rice paddy.

Sergt. Robert I. Hankinson, former banker and civilian pilot of Altoona, Pa., never got out. The ship had returned from an airstrip near a big field hospital.

The litter bearers, two stalwart GI's, picked up the litter on which the wounded Wisconsin Yank was lying and carried him to the waiting airship.

The wounded Yank looked up as he approached the ship. His eyes rested on the words painted on the L-5's nose, right near the propeller.

"The Wings of Mercy," the words read, "sponsored by the students of Redford Lutheran School."

I said I was from Detroit. "Great bunch of school kids out there," Sergt. Hankinson said. "They donated about 70 hospital evacuation ships to the southwest Pacific. Great bunch of kids."

He paused a moment and watched the wounded Yank being put into the ship. The litter bearers unlocked the sides behind the pilot. They fell down. Inside there was room for one litter. They laid the litter in carefully, tied it down.

"Hey," said the pilot, "hey, you from Detroit. Tell those kids back in your town this is a great ship. I cruise along at 100 to 105 miles an hour. I'll have this wounded lad in the hospital in 13 minutes flat, or I'm a fake!"

We backed away. The motor of the Wings of Mercy roared

She taxied down the airstrip and soared off into the sky. Exactly 20 minutes later the phone rang nearby, and somebody yelled, "Hey, is there a war correspondent down there?"

Sergt. Hankinson's voice came over the phone. "I told you so—13 minutes flat—you ought to see that wounded guy smile. Tell the kids back in Detroit about that, will you, pal?"

It was enough to make a civilian break into tears of emotion to watch the way the personnel at this airstrip operated.

The magnificent thing about all this is that if it were not for these mercy ships, the wounded would have to be driven four miles over rough, bumpy roads. I have gone over them by jeep, the rockiest roads in the world.

But the school children of Detroit took care of that! The patriotism of those youngsters, their money earned and saved, has saved the wounded from such rides.

In flew "The War Bond's Reward," an L-5 sponsored by the students of McFarlane School, Detroit, and, as a wounded platoon sergeant was loaded in I talked to the pilot, Sergt. Ted Diekert, of Houston, Tex.

"I got so interested in what those Detroit kids have done," he said, "that I wrote the school a letter. Jimminy, about a dozen of those schoolboys wrote back to me. I sure got a kick out of that. I'd give my right eye if they could see what these little ships of theirs are doing."

In came the "Pride of Salisbury," sponsored by the students of the Salisbury Elementary School, Detroit. I chatted for a moment with Staff Sergeant Robert H. Webb, of San Antonio, Tex., the pilot.

"I take The Pride up 2,000 to 3,000 feet," he said. "I go after smooth riding for my patients. I swing out over Lingayen Gulf, too, because it's smoother—and cooler."

He warmed up the ship's motor. I had timed it by my wrist watch. Two minutes after he landed, the Pride of Salisbury took off again.

"This is a sweet ship, old man," he said, and then the Pride of Salisbury flew off into the sky.

Ah, me, the school children of Detroit are a great bunch of kids. It's too bad they couldn't see what I saw today.

I know they would be happy.

« 29 »

Messman Makes Mess for Japs

As MAJ.-GEN. W. H. GILL, the divisional commander, pointed out, there is no safe place from the foothills of the Caraballo Mountains all the way up the Little Burma Road to the front lines on the Villa Verde Trail and the flanking mountain crests.

The other day the cavalry recon troop, resting near our camp, rushed out and killed nine Japs who had straggled down to the foothills.

The other night a group of us were sitting in a blacked-out Nipa hut, while a Signal Corps cameraman showed Richard Dix in "The Whistler." Our hero was about to swerve over a cliff with a beautiful doll, when the power went off. The field telephone rang. We were alerted for a Jap infiltration party of 50 supposed to have sneaked back into our lines.

The GI's pulled the bolts on their Garands. The officers released the safety catches on their automatics. A recon sergeant took his tommy-gun off his shoulder. We sat waiting in the dark, waiting. A GI said, "I wonder how that picture turned out?" We tried to guess what happened.

Nothing happened about the Jap infiltration party. Maybe some other Yanks knocked them off before they got to us; perhaps it was another Filipino rumor. For the Filipinos are always seeing a Jap behind every palm tree.

But the Filipinos are not always wrong!

Our camp is at Tayuk, a small Filipino town, where once the division fought hard to push the Nips up the Villa Verde Trail. The other day some Filipinos ran down the road toward our mess.

"Japs! Japs!" they shouted in terror.

Second Lieut. Alexander G. Miros, of 13507 Sparling avenue, Detroit, who runs a mess that serves 600 officers and enlisted men every day, was strolling down the dirt-street.

Now you wouldn't suppose Lieut. Miros, who I think runs the best mess I've yet encountered—you wouldn't think this capable mess officer was a fighting man.

But everybody in the 32nd fights in the Caraballo Mountains!

Lieut. Miros promptly rounded up a few idle Yank riflemen and a few more Filipino guerillas. He cross-examined the natives till he found out about where the Nips were last seen. He took his small band of men with him, with nothing but rifles, some grenades and his own automatic.

Well, this Detroiter who runs a fine mess also knows a lot about tactics. He directed a little military operation of his own. He spotted two Japs, armed with rifles and plenty of grenades, and then flanked them with his little group. The Japs opened up from their hideout in the tall grass near a river bed.

Lt. Miros' Yanks let them have it with grenades and rifle fire. The GI's got the first Jap in a few seconds. A few minutes later they had the second.

Returning to the mess to supervise the baking of pumpkin pies, Lieut. Miros said, "I got quite a bang out of it!"

I have eaten at a lot of mess set-ups in many divisions—in

France, England, Scotland, Ireland; in Oahu, Kwajalein, Saipan, Leyte, and in the Philippines. But I shall always believe Lieut. Miros runs the best mess anywhere.

His army career has been devoted to good food for his mess. He started out as a private in the Army, and worked his way up through all the non-com grades, finally becoming an officer.

When I visited his spic-and-span kitchen under canvas, with its 10 Army ranges and its detail of 28 men, I saw Mess Sergt. John Matz, 3511 Clippert street, Detroit, supervising the baking of 295 loaves of bread and 1,200 hot rolls.

Sergt. Frank L. Woo, of 16321 Warren avenue east, Detroit, is the first cook, and Pvt. Robert Winger, 20010 Canterbury Drive, Detroit, is a cook and baker.

The division was smart in putting these men at this work. Lieut. Miros worked in his father's cafe, and Sergt. Matz ran his own bakery back home, and Sergt. Woo owns an inn in Detroit.

The mess serves 80 gallons of coffee a meal, 200 pounds of fresh meat a day, including fried chicken from the states; 60 pounds of butter twice a week. Also ice-cold water at every meal, which is a luxury over here.

You may think I have been seeing moonbeams in my praise of this mess detail, especially you Red Arrow veterans of the last war, but here is a typical day's menu for three meals:

Breakfast: Ripe bananas, wheat cereal, hot cakes with syrup, bacon and coffee.

Lunch: Fried hamburgers, lyonnaise potatoes, stewed tomatoes, salad, fresh bread, bread pudding with lemon sauce, and cold tea.

Dinner: Soup, fried pork chops, sauerkraut, fresh corn on the cob (and tender, too!), salad, freshly baked rolls, chocolate cake with icing baked that afternoon, and hot coffee.

Lieut. Miros' lads in this mess are right on the beam, as the GI's say. Even the cooks shout, "How about seconds, boys?"

For myself, I hope I never get far away from this mess. I eat better here than I did back home at lunch in downtown Detroit!

« 30 »

Time Out to Jest

THE GI'S WERE LINED along the road, standing in the mud in their thick combat boots. The regimental band was playing a stirring air. With the American flag in front of them, and their blue company flags flying, the anti-tank cannon and headquarters companies of the 126th Infantry Regiment, marched by.

"They sure look sharp," a GI said, his rifle flung nonchalantly over his right shoulder.

After 73 days of hard fighting in the Ambayang River valley, on the left flank of the Little Burma Road, and on the Villa Verde Trail itself, the regiment had been pulled out of the line for some needed rest.

What had some of these fighting men, in the parade and on the sidelines, undergone? What were they thinking of now? Well, eight Detroit soldiers were sitting under a tree and since that's my home town, I thought there wasn't a finer opportunity to find out.

These Detroit soldiers looked rugged, with that lean, alert, sharp look of veterans who have met the Jap at 10 feet, hand to hand, and know that the war in the Pacific is far from over.

It was swell talking to them. They were so modest, laughing off tough experiences of war with a jest, talking about bullets and shell fragments that had narrowly missed them like it was something that happened to everybody.

My gosh, I had a swell time talking to these boys. I was lonesome anyway. I hadn't received a "sugar dispatch" from home since I got here. I took a little kidding about that. But it was all in fun.

I talked to Staff Sergt. Fred G. Hoffman, 14115 Hazelridge avenue, the sergeant major of the 2nd Battalion, 126th Infantry.

Sergt. Melvin R. Reiterman, 19369 Blake street, in a platoon of "pioneer and ammunition"; Pfc. George Jacob, 8124 Edgewood avenue, a machine gunner, and Pfc. Emerigileo Figliacconi, 18081 Riopelle street, a machine gunner.

Pvt. Anthony J. Lenkiewicz, 6025 Grandy avenue, of a "P & A" platoon; Pfc. Alex M. Galton, 1165 Harvard road, Grosse Pointe Farms, a rifleman.

Pfc. Leroy D. Freeman, 11700 Riad avenue, a gunner for a 37-mm. anti-tank gun; Sergt. Steve R. Kosuth, 6839 Miller avenue, a mortar squad leader.

Of course we talked about those 73 days they had been in the front lines, war that was always a hand's length near them, and in my notebook I recorded some of the conversation.

Hoffman: "The Jap artillery popped all around us up on the Villa Verde. I got pinned down a couple of times but I can spot a hole quickly, believe me."

Reiterman: "Our platoon ran rations back and forth to the line companies. Sometimes we acted as guides for Filipino carriers. Sometimes we had to carry boxes of rations on our backs, 200 yards . . . 300 yards . . . 400 yards. The Nips often opened up on us. Some of our boys took a beating from that fire."

Lenkiewicz: "Sometimes it was a thousand-yard haul. I was in a demolition squad. One day I sealed up a Jap cave. Had rifle cover. I circled around the cave, got on top of it, dropped a six-pound charge of TNT into it and pulled the fuse lighter. I had 25 seconds to get out of there—and boom!"

Jacob: "I was guarding the portable hospital up on the trail in my machine gun section. The Japs broke through one morning. One of our guards went to wake up his relief and found two Nips in his hole. Well, we wiped them out!"

Figliacconi: "Our machine gun section followed behind 'Fox' company while they were attacking up a slope. We took the hill, got kicked off twice by counterattacks, and then fought our way back for keeps."

Galton: "I was with a rifle platoon in 'Fox' company. You're not kidding, Figly, it was a tough fight. We fought up the slope, wormed our way around. I felt a few shots come close —oom!"

Reiterman: "Ever see a robot? That's us. We just fight our way automatically up a mountain peak. We don't think of nothing else but getting to the top."

Galton: "That's about all there is to it."

Kosuth: "Those guys carrying those heavy machine guns up those steep slopes do the work! Some of them carry 50 pounds, ouch!"

Freeman: "We haul our mountain gun up a hill the riflemen have taken and plaster the Japs on the next one. The riflemen come up the sides and we fire point blank into the middle. The rifle company phones us and tells us where to shoot. We knocked out a Jap 75-mm. mountain gun, too."

Reiterman: "I wouldn't believe it if I hadn't seen it."

Freeman: "Our gun has a lot of punch. The Jap 75 fired twice at our tanks. We spotted it in a draw and we poured 40 rounds into that baby. She never fired again."

Kosuth: "Our mortars stay about 300 yards back of a rifle company. I go with the combat patrol leader in the front lines."

"The patrol leader tells me where he wants the mortars laid down. I figure out the range. Over the field phone, I talk to the mortar section sergeant. I'll say, 'Five hundred yards one round!' I watch it. Then I might say, 'Bring it down to 400—20 miles to the left.'"

Kosuth broke into a big smile.

"And then," he said, hesitating.

"Tell him, Koss," said Freeman, "tell him."

Kosuth's smile was as big as they come.

"Well, then, sometimes, I say, 'Right on the button!'" said Kosuth.

Can you beat it?

« 31 »

Communiques Are Understatement

SOMETIMES I GET a big kick out of the terseness of our war communiques. They are brief and to the military pinpoint of tactics and strategy.

Yet often they are as impersonal as a lawyer's brief. Sometimes they remind me of the theme of that immortal poem, "All Quiet on the Potomac," dedicated to the GI's of another historic generation.

The last day, out of 73 long days and nights in the front lines of the Villa Verde campaign by the 2nd Battalion of the 126th Infantry Regiment, I thought one of our communiques was particularly terse.

I don't remember the exact words. They went something like this: "The fighting continued in Northern Luzon against isolated enemy garrisons."

What kind of fighting? What kind of action by fighting men that Gen. MacArthur inspires and leads?

I sat in the mud under a palm tree today with 18 Michigan combat soldiers, fresh out of the front lines. They knew the score.

For them it was a very personal war. For them the Jap was a close neighbor. You either killed him or he killed you. And what these Michigan men did, what they lived through, how they fought completely flabbergasted me.

After a long pull of lukewarm "chlorinated pop" from a canteen cup one of the boys offered me (the Philippine heat knocks me out), I asked Sergt. John Carskadon, of Grand Haven, Mich., "What happened to you up there that's interesting?"

"Oh, nothing much ever happens to me," said Sergt. Carskadon, "I go out on patrols and once a Jap put a 25 caliber bullet through my helmet. It only scratched my head. I haven't done so much."

Oh, yeah!

"I escort ration trains of carriers," said Pvt. Edward M. Coveny, of Grand Haven. "Sometimes the Jap snipers pick away at us."

"The Japs killed a couple of gunners on our machine gun," said Sergt. Thomas S. Raymond, of Romeo, Mich. "We got it out after dark. Had to save it. A squad leader crawled up and pulled it out, with Jap machine guns banging away at him."

"He was a big lad from Canton, with brass door knobs for a stomach," added Sergt. Joseph E. Harden, also of Grand Haven. "I was in that flareup."

The Japs were zeroed in on a machine gun operated by Pfc. Ronald V. Rowe, of Route No. 2, Jackson.

"We dug in on the reverse slope in the daytime," he said. "At night we would slip into our machine gun positions, crawl in and open up on them at daylight."

Sergt. Jack G. McAleer, of Mason, said he was glad to get

into "the fight again." Wounded in the left leg at Leyte, he is once more fit.

Staff Sergt. Edward D. Lowman, a platoon guide from Grand Haven, didn't look like he had been wounded in two campaigns. A phosphorus shell hit him in the right hand and chin at Leyte; a sniper put a bullet into his right leg at Buna.

An enemy shell hit 10 feet away from First Sergt. Richard J. Hansen, of Big Rapids, the "top kick" of "Easy" Company.

Staff Sergt. Frank W. Kiepnick, of Reed City, is a platoon guide for a rifle platoon. He takes patrols of six to fifteen men out close to the Jap lines. Sometimes the patrols "got too close and had to shoot their way out."

I talked to a switchboard operator for the battalion who loves his job, Pfc. Max S. Dewitt, of Route No. 5, Muskegon. "I hear a lot," he laughed, "so I know what's going on."

"When the Nip artillery drops some valentines," said Corp. Charles B. Stanley, 348 Youba street, Muskegon, a truck driver hauling supplies up to the front, "well, I take off on foot and dive for the nearest hole. There are plenty of them up in the mountains."

First Sergt. Donald L. Stout, 14 Meurer court, Muskegon, runs the enlisted men and the non-coms of "George" Company. "I make sure they're on the ball—and they always are!" he said.

"Our machine gun was supporting the riflemen," said Sergt. Steve Magiera, of Caro. "We were right up within a baseball toss of the Nips. They hollered and yelled at us all one night. Two tried to sneak into our lines, but the riflemen scored—bullseyes!"

"When we're carrying supplies right up into the line," said Staff Sergt. Edmund E. Rygiewicz, Caro, "the Jap snipers pop away. We hit the dirt, get up again, go ahead if all is quiet. Otherwise, we just keep jumping up, making a run for it, hitting the dirt—till we get up there."

Pfc. Lewis M. Watson, of 331 Michigan street, Grand Rapids, is a machine gunner who protected Yank outposts. Staff Sergt. Melvin O. Babcock, Stanton, said two gunners took turns, always behind their machine guns, night and day.

Pvt. William S. Trumble, of Ionia, is a runner for battalion headquarters. He was taking an order up to a company CP, when a shell landed 20 yards away. Untouched, he got up, and delivered the message.

A cook for the headquarters mess, like Pfc. Robert D. Carlson, 543 Stolpe avenue, Grand Rapids, does more than cook up forward on the Villa Verde. Carlson ran carrier ration trains up to the front lines.

"Our mortar section," said Pvt. Edward E. Hayes, 830 Jefferson avenue southeast, Grand Rapids, "goes right up back of the infantry companies all of the time. Our mortars keep the Japs from getting in at night."

So there you are.

That's what our Michigan boys are doing up on the Villa Verde.

« 32 »

Builders and Fighters Both

THE COMBAT ENGINEERS live a rugged life.

Two companies of the 114th Combat Engineers Battalion worked, fought, sweated it out on the Villa Verde trail, building a fine road over the footpath with the Japs banging away at them, night and day, with everything they had.

For 89 days these two companies were road builders on the

Villa Verde. Then they were pulled out of the front lines, sent back to the rear—to rebuild supply roads!

That's the way life is for the Combat Engineers.

They are the great work horses of the 6th Army. So I made a round trip of 140 miles by jeep, in the ever-present parboiling sun of Luzon, just to get the first-hand experience of some of the Michigan boys with these companies.

The hard ride, mostly over black dirt roads so bumpy they made your vertebrae feel like a hitching post for a balky mule; well, the long ride was worthwhile.

When you are a long way from home (10,600 miles in fact from downtown Detroit), it's fun to sit under a palm tree with some boys from back home.

Some of these things these Michigan boys have done, some of their experiences—well, they defy the imagination.

Our boys make fine soldiers. And they like to sit around and talk about the war the way ball players compare notes after a 12-inning baseball game. Only this is a bigger game, for keeps, with the lives of our Yanks always at stake.

So six of us from grand old Michigan sat around "shooting the breeze." With me were:

Pfc. Edward J. Gostomski, 11466 Klinger avenue, Hamtramck, a rifleman who walked behind an armored bulldozer on the Villa Verde Trail, popping away at Jap snipers.

Sergt. Frank L. Van Steenkiste, of Fraser, Mich., another rifle guard for the Villa Verde armored bulldozer.

Corp. Kenneth C. Hutchison, of Harbert, Mich., who blasted out giant rocks on the Villa Verde with TNT charges, a dangerous job, but Corp. Hutch was up to it!

Corp. Gilbert E. Blakeslee, of 300 Fifty-second street, Grand Rapids, a mechanic, who dug up Jap mines on the Villa Verde, one of those engineering jobs that requires patience, tense alertness and courage.

Pfc. Albert B. Grappin, of Essexville, Mich., driver of a two and one-half ton truck that hauled logs, supplies and engineers up the hairpin turns of the Villa Verde.

Corp. Laudy W. Harrison, 509 Hazelton avenue, Flint, who repaired machine guns and bazookas for the engineers.

When you get with fighting men like these, after chinning about things back home as a warm-up, you are always tempted to ask, "Well, fellows what's new and interesting that happened to you up front?"

So I pitched the question out.

Hutchison: "It's just a lot of hard work up there. Road building under fire is no picnic. You can be working on a revetment with a shovel—but you've always got your rifle on your back, ready.

"A Jap artillery dud lit within 12 feet of me. It might as well have let go. Honestly, I was half scared to death for a minute. So I popped away at a sniper, just to keep my nerves in hand."

Van Steenkiste: "The Japs had some .75 mountain guns up on the trail. They peppered away at our armored cab. But our artillery's counter-battery work is good. In my job, we watch out for Jap snipers. One Jap at the corner of the trail had us covered with a machine gun. I dropped flat on my puss. He had us pinned down. Then the infantry patrols came out and killed him with rifle fire."

Gostomski: "We were always running into the Japs at the water points. They fought hard for them. Once we took a water point, we had to set up a perimeter defense and get ready for a lot of counterattacks. But we are good at defending those water points."

Van Steenkiste: "I had to go it alone for three hours one day behind the dozer. You have to keep on your toes."

Hutchison: "The Japs are always trying infiltration into us at night. You don't get much rest up there, but you kill a lot of them."

Blakeslee: "I was 25 yards in front of a tractor when it got hit by a mine. The mine threw it up on the left side of the road. Then I dug up a 1,000-pound mine ahead of it. If the tractor had hit that baby, it would have blown it over the cliff."

Grappin: "I was driving on the Villa Verde with a load of gravel. A GI hollered, 'They're some Japs over there!' So we took 10 minutes off and killed three."

Harrison: "Up there on the trail, we work, duck bullets and mortars—and keep on working. Sometimes we work 12 hours a day. We work in our steel helmets, with our rifles and ammo always handy. It's hot work building a road in a steel helmet, but I'm always glad to have one on."

Van Steenkiste: "Anything can happen. I was right behind a bulldozer when it went over a cliff. The driver jumped out. The dozer rolled down 300 feet. That was close enough for me."

Now you know why I like the Combat Engineers so much. They are doing a great job on the Villa Verde!

« 33 »

Manila Bares A Wounded Heart

THERE ARE SOME things which seem unrelated at the time, which often determine what a man will do.

For there seems no connection among the seven GI's who went to Manila with me to broadcast for Radio Station WWJ-The Detroit News, and the three little Filipino girls who sang for us in the foothills of the Caraballo Mountains, and Alex, the fighting Filipino, twice wounded on the Villa Verde Trail.

You would say these were unrelated things. Yet, were they? Because of them I spent three nights and two days in the Sam

Miguel slum district of Manila to learn something about the Filipinos for whom so many Yanks of the 32nd Division had died up in the Caraballo Mountains.

I couldn't forget those three little girls. A judge gave a party in a private school where only English is spoken and American history is taught with gusto.

The party was by candlelight. The three little girls—they were 3, 5 and 7 years old—got up to sing. They were very cute, like little brown dolls, and the smallest one had the face of an angel.

With two score GI's listening, their Army flashlights providing impromptu spotlights, these little girls sang in English, "Ole Black Joe," "Oh, Susanna" and "Carry Me Back to Ole Virginny." And when they sang "God Bless America" the GI's almost tore down the thatched building with applause.

Sometime later, Lieut.-Col. Charles R. (Monk) Meyer, a young West Pointer who is one of the best battalion commanders in the Army, told me about Alex.

Alex just joined up with "Easy" Company of the 127th Infantry Regiment. For some reason Alex didn't want to fight with the Filipino guerillas. For reasons of his own, Alex hated the guerillas. But Alex was a first-class fighting man. The GI's gave him a Garand a dead Yank would never use again and fitted him out as a GI combat soldier.

All through the Villa Verde campaign this little Filipino, about 5 feet 2 inches in height and 125 pounds in weight, has fought with the Yanks. Twice wounded, he twice went AWOL from evacuation hospitals in the rear, hitch-hiking back to "Easy" Company.

"Me, 'Easy' Company Joe," Alex said.

When you heard Col. Meyer talk about Alex, and when you heard those three little girls sing, you knew there was more to the Filipinos than the surface showed. Men and women who go barefooted and sleep on the floor must have character, courage and thoughts, too, and what are they?

So, when the broadcast was over, I decided to go down into the slums and live there a few days. I know Sergt. Melvin R. Reiterman, of 19369 Blake street, Detroit, thought I was a bit wacky. He said so.

I met Sergio Acuram, an attorney, whom we promptly called Tony. He ran a store for PCAU (the Philippine Civilian Affairs Unit of the American Army), which the GI's call Peekow. His wholesale warehouse keeps 20,000 people in the slum area from starving.

There is an unseen Providence which seems to protect the poor of Manila and their chief industry, children. Although bombs and artillery and Jap dynamite had devastated the beautiful part of the once-modern city of Manila, the slums were almost untouched by war.

So refugees from all other districts, who had no homes to go to, descended on the poor people, and the poor took them in. As a result, these people of the slums were packed together like K rations.

Tony got me a bed with five other Filipinos sleeping in the same room in a nipa-house. I went around the neighborhood talking to the people. It was amazing that most of them spoke English; it was almost pathetic how much they liked the GI's.

And swarms of GI's roamed around the neighborhood, on three-day passes from the front, because of the welcome they found here; a genuine, warm welcome from the hearts of people who had nothing but their courage.

There was little plumbing in the neighborhood. The sewers were open-air affairs, tiny ditches running down both sides of the streets. In some places there were open cesspools. The slums were in a one-time swamp district. The mosquitoes were thick and the bullfrogs put up such a roar at night that they sounded like an orchestra of bass drums.

Life was very much in the primitive state, but somehow the people managed to keep clean, to laugh, to have a good time.

Tony threw a party for the GI's of the Red Arrow Division. It was a swell party. Nine Filipinos came over as a dance orchestra and played American jazz on their banjos and guitars.

Then the girls came with their mothers and their older sisters and their aunts as chaperones. They danced with the GI's. Tony loves to make speeches. He made at least five on "How happy we are the Americans are here."

So I lived with these people. I slept in their little homes, swatted mosquitoes with them and ate their food. Up through the poverty and the inconveniences there seeped a great admiration for them.

Despite their poverty, they were happy. PCAU sold them canned sardines for 8 cents, salmon for 10 cents, 10 ounces of rice for 2 cents, sugar for 10 cents a pound, canned milk for 15 cents, canned beef for 50 cents a pound, vegetables for 24 cents a pound. PCAU kept them alive.

"We all have enough to eat now, thanks to the Americans," Tony said.

Finally, I left the neighborhood and lived with some Army officers; slept on a good Army cot under a capable mosquito bar and ate good Army food. It was more like living.

And then I met Lieut. John Phelps, of the 120th Anti-Aircraft, who lived with Glenn Richards, DPW commissioner of Detroit, during summers at Walnut Lake, 20 miles out of Detroit. He is the former music director for Cass Technical High School.

"It's rugged down in the slums," Phelps said. "You shouldn't have tried it. Only the Filipinos can stand it down there."

« 34 »

"The Little Man of Football"

Gus Dorais, city councilman in Detroit and coach of the Detroit Lions, always had a soft spot in his heart for the little men of football because Gus is a little fellow himself.

So in 1937, when Gus was coaching the College All-Stars for their impending game in Chicago with the Green Bay Packers, he stood talking with Monk Meyer, the star halfback for the Army. Monk was a member of his squad.

"Don't work too hard in practice, Monk," Dorais said. "I'm not going to put you in the game. Green Bay is a bunch of huskies—and I'm afraid you will get hurt!"

Did you ever wonder, Gus, what happened to Monk Meyer, who sat on the bench beside you during that game?

Well, Lieut.-Col. Charles R. (Monk) Meyer, commander of the 2nd Battalion of the 127th Infantry Regiment, is one of the great fighting men of this war!

Monk Meyer is a legendary figure now in the Red Arrow Division. The GI's call him "a good Joe." Maj.-Gen. W. H. Gill, commander of the 32nd, said he was "a great leader of men."

This so-called "little man of football," who didn't play for Gus Dorais because he "might get hurt," has won two Silver Stars for gallantry in combat, a Bronze Star for heroic achievement under fire, and two Purple Hearts for wounds received in action.

When I first went up to the front, a dozen GI's said the same thing to me, "Have you seen The Monk yet? What a guy!"

A big lanky soldier from Nebraska told me, as we sat in a

hillside cave: "He's tops—that Monk. Brother, in Leyte we were fighting the Japs down a road. The Monk was walking out in front of his men, his 45 blazing, picking Japs off right and left. By gosh, what a guy!"

I saw Monk a few days after his latest achievement. The entire division was talking about it. Monk was currently out of action. He had blown up a Jap cave with five Nips inside blazing at him—and set the charge so well he blew himself off his feet. The Monk lost an eardrum in that affair.

I had a bad cold and I was "sweating it out" on an Army cot when in came Monk and sat down to talk about Gus Dorais and the old days at West Point.

He didn't look much like a fighting officer. He wears rimmed glasses and he never swears. He always says "Dad gum" about everything. He looked very lean and slight. His 145 pounds just doesn't fill out his frame. He is 5 feet 11.

"I hear you blew yourself up with a charge of TNT," I said.

Lt.-Col. Meyers laughed, one of those low laughs that has the swish of a Jap saber in it.

"Dad gum," said Monk, "I got a little mad out there. I had all sorts of trouble that day. I was out with one of my patrols sealing Nip caves. Those Nips would push our TNT charges back out of the holes, or roll them out. It just got my goat, that's all. After that there wasn't much to it. I'm afraid some of my boys have been telling you fairy tales."

Monk was a bit modest.

What happened was this:

Monk and his party were approaching two Jap caves that were protecting each other with supporting fire. A hidden Jap machine gun opened up on Monk's patrol, wounding four soldiers beside him. So Monk went on alone.

He crawled up on top of a Jap cave. He could hear the Japs talking inside. With some wire he dropped a grenade at the entrance of the cave. It didn't go off!

He crawled back to his own lines, came back with another charge. Again, it failed to go off. For the third time he went back, this time with a six-pound charge of TNT, lowered it down by wire, pulled the igniter fuse, and blew up the cave and the Japs.

"Dad gum," said Monk, "you should have seen me sweating it out on top of that cave. Every now and then that other cave would pop away at me with a machine gun."

Lieut.-Col. Meyer then got a flame thrower and some soldiers with grenades, and they burnt out the Japs in the second cave. There was one more cave nearby. It had to be sealed before dark. Monk volunteered to go it alone.

He crawled for 20 yards under rifle and machine gun fire to get up to the cave. He approached it from one side. When he was in position to set the charge in the cave, Monk pulled the fuse lighter on the TNT and held it in his hand while the fuse burned low.

"I didn't want to give those Nips a chance to kick it out," he explained.

Then he reached in, set the TNT in the cave, and was promptly disgusted.

"The dad gum thing rolled over," Monk said. "I thought the fuse would go out. So I reached in and turned it over. It was okay, still burning. I ducked and boom! It let go."

The charge knocked Monk over and broke an eardrum in his right ear. But the cave was sealed and another group of Japs were dead. A soldier started hollering, "Medics! Medics! Col. Meyer is hit!"

His men came rushing over to him, heedless of the enemy in the brush, for they love Monk. But Col. Meyer jumped up, shook himself.

"Dad gum," he said, "I'm all right. Let's get some chow!"

So now you know, Gus Dorais, why Monk Meyer, the little

man of football who sat on your bench in the All-Star game of 1937, is a legendary figure on the Villa Verde Trail.

Fighting men don't come any better than Monk Meyer—and some day Charles Robert Meyer, Jr., the eight-month-old son he has never seen, will be very proud of his dad.

« 35 »

119 Grueling Days

IN THE ONE HUNDRED and nineteenth day of fighting, the veteran 32nd Division broke the back of the stubborn Jap resistance on the Villa Verde Trail.

Maj.-Gen. W. H. Gill, division commander, informed the 6th Army Command that the Villa Verde campaign had been won. For the Red Arrow Division fought its way through the mountains to the little town of Imugan, not much of a town in size, but of tactical importance in the campaign.

The rugged men of the division smashed Jap resistance on Hill 527 and Hill 528, and in the Salacsac Pass. The Japs retreated down the Imugan River Valley.

They had slugged it out for those 119 days with the 32nd, and taken a trouncing. The division's veterans killed 8,850 Japs and took only 50 prisoners. So bitter was the fighting that it took the division four months to fight its way 25 miles through the mountains.

* * * * *

A number of Detroit and Michigan soldiers fought through this campaign, which still goes on in the mopping-up phase.

Our boys always like the Filipino children. The other morning 10-year-old Rebecca Obana carried her four-year-old brother into the portable hospital.

The Japs had ambushed 50 Filipino civilians trying to reach

our lines, cutting them down with machine guns. The Filipino lad had a scalp wound. The girl had a wound in her arm.

An Ohio medic took care of the boy. But Sergt. Roy H. Moerschell and Pfc. George H. Neubacher, both of Detroit, patched up the girl. Moerschell bandaged her arm; Neubacher improvised a sling.

* * * * *

Some Filipinos shouted and waved to Sergt. Eugene Sprecher, 9236 Kresge, Detroit, while Sprecher and a companion walked down a narrow trail. "Two Japs," the Filipinos said.

Sprecher and his friend searched the tall kunai grass. One of the Nips stood up. The Yanks fired and he fell over dead.

* * * * *

High up on the Villa Verde, Sergt. James C. Crucian, 4655 Russell, Detroit, was awarded the Bronze Star for meritorious achievement in action in the earlier fighting in Leyte.

During bitter action, a number of wounded Yanks were pinned down by enemy fire. Crucian crawled across the terrain, with enemy machine gun bullets popping around him. He crept from wounded man to wounded man, treating them all. He was credited with saving the lives of at least four.

* * * * *

The M Seven, a 105 howitzer on a full track, was under direct fire by a Jap anti-tank gun and a mountain gun. But the M Seven advanced at the gun positions, with shrapnel richocheting above the heads of the tank men. The M Seven blasted out the Jap guns and the ground defenses of the enemy around them crumbled.

For his part in this action, Corp. Harold Bargowski, 40816 Chase road, Belleville, Mich., was awarded the Bronze Star.

* * * * *

Pfc. Jerome J. Michalski, of 6246 Evaline, Detroit, has been awarded the Purple Heart for wounds received in the Villa Verde. Now completely recovered, he is back with his unit.

The battlefield gives many heretofore unsung soldiers opportunities to show capacities for leadership. The division is always quick to reward such soldiers with battlefield promotions.

It is a long jump from a non-com rating to second lieutenant, but two Detroiters made it.

For "superior performance in combat," Alan F. Burkland, of 15021 Fairfield, Detroit, was promoted from staff sergeant to second lieutenant.

For "recognition of his outstanding services and leadership," Carl J. Heinrichs, 145 Tyler, Highland Park, was promoted from staff sergeant to second lieutenant.

Dominick W. Wasukonis, of 3680 Trombly, Detroit, and Robert F. Jeffrey, of 3138 Canfield east, Detroit, were promoted from privates first class to sergeants.

Robert J. Morris, 9449 Henley, Detroit, was advanced from sergeant to staff sergeant; Stanley M. Kroll, 1409 Blaine, Detroit, from private first class to corporal; Raymond C. Davio, 7656 Puritan, Detroit, from staff sergeant to first sergeant.

Medic Chester J. Rutkowski, 3916 Norwalk, Hamtramck, from private first class to corporal; Medic Robert Diebolt, 1841 Leslie, Detroit, from private first class to corporal.

* * * *

The Commonwealth of the Philippines continues to show its gratitude to Detroit soldiers for their part in liberating Northern Luzon.

The following 11 Detroiters received the Philippine Liberation Medal today:

Pfc. Wilford D. Hobson, 1341 Holbrook; Pvt. Michael Grudzinky, 7442 Grandville; Pfc. Alex Galton, 1165 Harvard road, Grosse Pointe Park; Pfc. Peter J. Sind, 8058 Knodell.

Sergt. Joseph G. Leithelm, 4946 Lawndale; Corp. Charles N.

Monssean, 550 Dickerson; Pvt. Vernon J. Miller, 1603 Lemay; Sergt. Lawrence S. Rady, 12031 Kentucky; Sergt. Fred G. Hoffman, 14115 Hazelridge.

Pfc. Alex Tkachuk, 11700 St. Louis; Pfc. Craig L. Rayl, 159 Richter, River Rouge.

* * * * *

For exemplemary behavior in combat these six Detroiters have received the Combat Infantryman's Badge:

Pvt. William J. Stoelton, 3587 Sixteenth; Pvt. Charles B. Glisson, 140 Pingree; Pvt. Stanley J. Baharski, 6029 Braden: Pfc. Edward E. Campbell, 9705 American; Pvt. Leo J. Gorecki, 6236 Sheridan; Pvt. James C. Hennessee, Jr., 5826 Rohns.

The Good Conduct Medal has been awarded to Pfc. Elmer D. Riew, 12284 Goulburn; Pfc. Walter J. Mydlak, Jr., 7511 Prairie; Sergt. Dominick W. Wasukonis, 3680 Trombly; Sergt. George J. Lehman, 5765 Maxwell.

* * * * *

There are a number of Red Arrow veterans now entering their fourth year overseas with the division. Soldiers like Pfc. LaVerne C. Foss, 203 Main west, Belding; Pfc. Walter Janick, 4826 Martin, Detroit; Sergt. Frank W. Kimmel, 6245 Helen, Detroit, and Pfc. Charles J. Keough, 3777 Longfellow, Detroit.

* * * * *

Four Detroiters newly assigned to the division are Pvt. Thomas B. Kirkaldy, Jr., 799 Eastlawn; Pvt. Chester T. Kudlaczyk, 7417 Faust; Pvt. Charles R. Glissen, 140 Pingree, and Pfc. Edward E. Campbell, 9705 American.

« 36 »

Not One Remained Alive

THERE WAS AN ODOR of death in and around the Kongo Fortress. Jap bodies still lay sprawled in sudden death on the mountain side. A detail of Yanks was busy burying Japs on the crest.

For the Red Arrow Division killed from 1,000 to 1,100 Japanese here. The division called it Hill 508; the enemy called it the Kongo Fortress, and thought it was impregnable. For Hill 508 is the highest and steepest of the hills on the flanks of the Villa Verde Trail.

The division approached the Kongo on March 20 from the south. The drive stopped because it was difficult evacuating the wounded and getting up supplies from that direction. Later the division started a drive on the hill from the north.

It was a hard fight. The Japs decided to make a stand on the Kongo to the last man. For three weeks, 24 hours a day, the fight went on. The division stormed the hill, but not until every Jap was dead.

What made the Kongo so difficult to capture was the fact that it was a great underground fortress dug deep into the hillside.

The fortress was built around 25 feet below the crest. It was cut through the slopes on both sides, about 150 feet long and 100 feet wide.

The entrances were small manholes, only big enough for a soldier to crawl into. Then they opened up into tunnels, high enough so a Jap could stand erect in them and walk through. The fortress was built with a main tunnel, and large tunnel-rooms off it in the shape of L's and K's.

At one end there was a giant room where officers slept; at the other another similar-sized underground room where the enlisted men slept. Machine guns protected the entrances. These were braced with timbers, like mine entrances in the states.

I crawled up the steep slope of the Kongo with Sergt. Loring N. Black, Jr., of Brooklyn, and Pvt. Theodore B. Metzger, of 4973 Cabot street, Detroit. There is a little mountain goat in Teddy Metzger. He got far ahead of us. My heart was pounding in my throat as we climbed up, hanging on to tree trunks and skinny bushes on the ascent.

Our mortars were clamoring away up on the crest. They sounded like thunder. I almost walked on a Jap soldier's head on the way up. Teddy pointed to a Jap skull.

"Our boys sure currycombed this position with artillery, mortars, machine guns, grenades and TNT charges," Sergt. Black said. "There's nothing left."

Modern warfare has erased every tree, blown up the bushes, scraped the slopes clean of moss and grass. Up on the crest I saw Pvt. Robert O. Marx, of 1226 Second street west, Flint, looking through a mountain periscope.

"You get a swell view up here," he said.

He showed me how to operate the giant 'scope as I sat down behind it, with a sheer drop of 1,500 feet below me. Overlooking us were Mt. Imugan and hills still held by the Japs, hills they call Pheasant and Wind and Rain.

"Sometimes you can see a Jap soldier prowling around on Imugan," Pvt. Marx said.

I watched our white phosphorous shells dropping on the slopes and crest of Imugan. Below was the broad Imugan river valley, and looking toward the left I saw the beautiful Cagayan valley, looking so flat and inviting from this height.

Far in the distance were the Sierra Madre Mountains. In the other direction was Highway Five, twisting and turning down from the Balete Pass on into Santa Fe. On our flank, I could see elements of the 25th Division moving forward. The Villa Verde itself was masked by Hill 526.

For a moment there was a bit of action. An M-7, a 105 on a full track, was moving forward. It stopped. Fired a few rounds at the Japs up ahead.

I turned around and almost fell into a deep trench the Japs had dug. I crawled over and watched our boys burying the Jap dead. They showed me the entrances to the Kongo, which brave Yanks had sealed with heavy charges of TNT. Then the Yanks dug open the big cave, found 52 dead Japs at one entrance, and resealed it.

I crawled over on the crest and sat down to talk with Pfc. Jack Stilson, 18745 Grandville avenue, Detroit, who has been fighting with his machine gun section in the Caraballo Mountains for 80 days.

"I made that deep hole," he said. He pointed to it, behind us. "Kind of home made. Then I put my poncho over it. The Japs have been firing at us up here with their mountain guns. It gets a little hot."

We chinned for awhile about Mayor Jeffries, Council President Lodge; the pigeons at the City Hall, the bench sitters in Grand Circus Park; about nostalgic things like that, so far away.

Then our little party fought its way down the steep slope, slowly, at a crawl, sometimes on all fours. In our jeep we started back down the Little Burma Road to our camp on the mountainside.

We saw a tired soldier and offered him a lift. Sergt. Carl Leichwise, 146 Ferris avenue, Highland Park, attached to a medical battalion, was grateful. He had a day's furlough in the foothills and he was trying to hike it. We stopped a truck going back to the rear and got him a lift.

"Say hello to Detroit for me," said Sergt. Leichwise.

We passed the hillside portable hospital. Only a few minutes before Maj. Gen. W. H. Gill, the division commander, had stood beside a two-year-old Filipino boy on the operating table. A Jap hand grenade had killed his parents and broken his left arm. The GI's rescued him and the medics saved his life.

The general patted him on the head, and the small Filipino boy alone, among strangers, unable to speak a word of English, smiled back.

"He's a cute little fellow," Gen. Gill had said.

« 37 »

"Little Boy" Leads the Way

THE FOG WAS CLEARING up in the Caraballo Mountains. It had hung like a heavy smoke cloud around the mountain peaks. Then the sunrise seeped through and slowly the fog faded out.

A squadron of Thunderbolts roared through the clouds and out into the open sky above us. I was standing on the Villa Verde Trail, at the edge of a steep cliff, with radio headphones at my ears.

Capt. William P. David, of Monterey, Calif., was in charge of our radio party that Pfc. William Fleming, of 301 Bayside south, Detroit, had driven up the trail at 6 a. m. It was, incidentally, very cold. We wore our ponchos to keep warm.

Capt. David had a vital job. The air strikes were set up to knock out Jap positions. It was the California captain's job to "talk the Thunderbolts into the target," so no "eggs" fell within our lines. Sometimes that has happened in both theaters of war.

The Thunderbolts looked beautiful in the sun. Capt. David grabbed a radio telephone mike. From now on I am going to record some conversation, but the code words I will change. None of the code words are genuine, but they will give you an idea the way it is done.

Capt. David said, "This is Music Box Special calling Michigan Red Leader."

The squadron leader's voice was clear and crisp.

"This is Michigan Red Leader to Music Box Special, go ahead, please."

David: "You are directly over our troops, over our troops. Your target is eight miles northwest, northwest."

Red Leader: "Roger. Just flew above Balete Pass."

David: "Your target will be marked by Little Boy . . . a Little Boy."

("Little Boy" is the amusing nickname of the dive bombers for the L-5 which directs and guides mountain bombing missions for the safety of our troops.)

Red Leader: "Where is Little Boy, Little Boy?"

David: "This is Music Box Special calling Little Boy."

Suddenly, up out of the draw between two mountains, we saw the L-5 in the haze. It seemed to be walking through the air, compared to the speed of the Thunderbolts.

Our troops were moving about on the slope above us, watching the dive bombers, smiling. They knew that each dive bomber carried 2,000-pound bombs.

We heard Little Boy talking to Red Leader:

"Take your message up to Six (height of 6,000 feet)."

"Well, they've contacted Little Boy," Capt. David told me, as a thousand Filipino carriers went by in a long column, carrying water and food and ammo on their shoulders.

We heard a pilot say, "I see Little Boy (indicating direction), at 2 o'clock."

Little Boy: "The target is right below me. Overcast is thick. Trying to find an opening to get in . . . no opening . . . Try secondary target (and, minutes later:) It is overcast too."

Red Leader: "Get me something, will you, pal? We've got some beautiful eggs, some big ones, and we don't want to take them home."

Little Boy: "Will do."

David to Pfc. Fleming: "He's a bloodthirsty gent, that leader."

"Those Thunderbolt pilots sure like to help out the infantry," said Fleming. Then turning to me: "They're great guys."

The Thunderbolts cruised around, flying in giant circles overhead. The Japs usually opened up on our positions at this hour. Now they were very quiet.

Fleming scrounged a canteen cup of hot coffee, and we made a loving cup out of it. Nobody had had any breakfast, yet. Later, we ate K rations.

Little Boy found a good target. The town of Koyaga Proper in the mountains beyond us had ration dumps, ammunition, supplies; it was lined with caves full of Jap troops. The L-5 took the Thunderbolts over it.

"I see a lot of Nips down there, Mike," one pilot said to another. "What they need are a few of our valentines."

Red Leader: "How is Atlanta (a cold name substituted by me for the real one that means weather)?"

Little Boy: "It's okay."

Red Leader: "Have you on right, at 2 o'clock. Are you going to put Joe Doakes (a white phosphorus drop) on the target?"

Little Boy: "Here it goes."

Red Leader: "Have target in sight, a little knob on the hill. Will make a dry run for size." (A dry run is a dive without dropping a bomb.)

Little Boy, later: "Right on the button."

Red Leader: "I'm going into a dive now. I will make two passes. Here I go."

There was a roar over the radio. I looked up and saw the Thunderbolt peel out of formation. It dove straight down, thousands of feet, with a roar like a thundering locomotive.

A GI up on our hill roared, "Whoopee!"

"I don't think he's coming out of his dive," Fleming said.

There was a terrific roar of the big bomb hitting.

"There he is again," David said. "He's making the second pass."

We saw another flight of 12 Thunderbolts flying near us. Another leader said to Little Boy, "Am I to follow Michigan in?"

Little Boy: "Stand by."

The Thunderbolts in the first formation were ready.

"Get out of your swivel chair Doodle Bug," one pilot said, "and go on in."

"Okay, Muscles," said the pilot's voice over the radio. "Here I go."

The Thunderbolts made their bomb runs. That was a beautiful sight. They peeled off, one at a time, and, seconds later, terrific explosions were heard. Tall columns of smoke came up from the Jap positions.

Red Leader: "This is Michigan Red Leader to Little Boy. How did we do? How did we do? The show is over."

Little Boy: "That was a very good job. Excellent. You were right on the target. Right on the button."

Red Leader: "Thanks, pal. We'll go home, now."

Little Boy: "This is Little Boy calling Detroit Red Leader (the second flight). Go in now. Go in now."

Detroit Red Leader: "Okay, Little Boy, here I go."

Sometime later, DRL.: "Were those bombs on the target?"

Little Boy: "Right on the button."

DRL: "Thanks, pal."

More columns of smoke were rising from the Jap target area. Our Thunderbolts turned around and went rambling home, the sun shining brightly on their burnished sides. A GI rifleman, from Texas it developed, his helmet caked with mud, came strolling down the Villa Verde.

"Nice show, Joe," I said.

"Swell show, Joe," he said. "Those Thunderbolts are a good deal for the infantry. A good deal."

« 38 »

How They Got Their Stars for Gallantry

AFTER BREAKFAST one morning, Maj.-Gen. W. H. Gill, commander of the Red Arrow Division, said to me, "I'm going to decorate three Detroit soldiers this morning."

He paused for a moment while he scratched Ramrod, his police dog, behind the ear.

"They're good fighting men, these three boys," he said.

I sat around waiting for them to report. About an hour later they lined up in battle dress, their herringbone twills well worn from front-line foxholes; their helmets a bit muddy.

Gen. Gill stood straight as a ramrod at one side. Beside him stood Col. E. A. Barlow, of Salt Lake City, Utah, the division's chief of staff. Lieut.-Col. George A. Bond, Jr., of San Angelo, Tex., a division staff officer, read the citations.

At attention stood Sergt. Herman J. Fritz, 13319 Prest; Master Sergt. Lawrence R. Ortkras, 8847 Pinehurst, and Sergt. Robert H. Miley, 5026 Third, all of Detroit.

Our boys stood at attention as if their backs were made of marble pillars. The veins in their necks stood out a little. It isn't every day that a soldier is decorated by his General, and all the boys in this division like Gen. Gill.

The citations over, Col. Bond stepped back. The General pinned the Silver Star for gallantry in action on the left breast of Fritz. Then he stepped back, thrust out his hand, and they shook hands.

"Congratulations, Fritz," said Gen. Gill. "Grand job."

Then he pinned the Bronze Star ribbons on Ortkras and Miley and shook hands with them. Col. Barlow also shook hands with them and spoke further words of commendation. Col. Bond did likewise.

I joined the boys and we looked at Fritz' Silver Star. It is a very beautiful medal.

"It looks swell," said Miley.

"I guess I'd better send it home," Fritz said.

So I asked them to "step into my office," a little patch of grass on the hillside. We talked about what they had done.

Sergt. Fritz is a lean, tough-looking squad leader, fully recovered from a piece of grenade shrapnel which wounded him in the right arm, and from 37 pieces of grenades which lodged in his body from his ankles up into his back.

"I am with 'Charley' Company of the 127th Infantry," Fritz said. " 'Able' Company had a patrol out on the Villa Verde, on a river bed. It had a hot fight with the Nips; lost two men killed. They tried for two days to get those men out.

"That's the difference between our Army and the Japs—one of the differences. They let the bodies of their men rot on the hillsides. We always see our boys get a decent burial."

Sergt. Fritz took a long pull on a cigaret.

"I'm for that, 100 per cent," he said. "All of us fighting out there know that, if anything happens, the division won't leave us. Some of our boys will go out and get us."

So "Charley" Company relieved "Able" Company in this action. A lieutenant took out a patrol the first morning to get the bodies of the two Yanks. Fritz said they worked their way up through the hills and bivouacked at night in the Kunai grass near the Jap lines.

They were in the river bed the next morning. The lieutenant said, "Sergt. Fritz, can you make it up the hill where the bodies are?"

"I'll try," Fritz said.

With five guerillas, Fritz started up the steep slope. It took them two hours to climb it. It was a climb at a 60-degree angle. Once Fritz slipped and rolled down the hill. Finally, they reached the dead Yanks.

They put the bodies in ponchos, and started to carry them down. The Nips opened up, the citation read; Fritz and his little party fought their way back with the two dead Yanks. It was a long, hard trek.

And this is what the division meant when it gave Fritz a Silver Star for gallantry in action. He risked his life that two Yanks could have a decent burial in the Army cemetery in the foothills of the Caraballo Mountains.

Sergt. Miley, now a medical technician, was an ambulance driver on the Villa Verde for a month. He was cited for meritorious achievement, for driving the wounded down the Villa Verde at night, without lights, his ambulance sliding in the mud, always under enemy fire.

This night ambulance driving is hard on the nerves, but Miley is nerveless. One night the rain caused a landslide on the Villa Verde. With four seriously wounded patients, he got his ambulance through the huge pile of mud and dirt, with two wheels on the edge of the cliff.

It took him four hours to go three miles that night!

Master Sergt. Ortkras won his meritorious achievement citation by less spectacular, but just as important methods. He is the 127th's regimental motor supply officer. Throughout the campaign on the Villa Verde he kept 43 big trucks feeding ammo, water, supplies and troops up the Villa Verde.

One convoy of trucks, led by Ortkras, hauled 42 tons of ammunition to the front lines, under fire, too, in one day.

He packed 375 Filipino carriers into five trucks one day and rushed them to the front. The medics needed "daisy chain" litter bearers.

So that is how these three Detroiters won their medals and the commendation of their General as he pinned them on.

« 39 »

Villa Verde is a Panorama of War

OUR HEAVY MORTARS were making a terrific racket from the hill above me. Down in the valley our heavy howitzers were throwing up a barrage. Overhead Thunderbolts were speeding through the sky.

There is a vast uproar about war. There is a giant panorama of ceaseless activity. Company runners coming from battalion. Litter bearers carrying the wounded. Filipino carriers in long columns carrying supplies. Ambulances. Trucks. Patrols on the hillsides.

On the hillsides overlooking the trail, far to the right and far to the left, there is a continuous rattle of machine guns and small-arms fire. A Garand makes a loud, determined crack. The Jap weapons, lighter, make a popping sound.

I changed jeeps three times that day on the Villa Verde, a sort of anxious hitch-hiker, always half scared to death by gun-fire. Finally, I took a long hike with a Lansing officer.

I had been on the trail about five hours, and Col. Merle H. Howe, of Grand Rapids, veteran commander of the 128th Infantry, sent a runner after sandwiches. Steak sandwiches and hot coffee revive your spirits.

These full colonels of the Red Arrow are real fighting men. No "feather merchants" among them. (A "feather merchant" is GI slang for a rear echelon officer.)

There were five full colonels in the division. In this campaign, one was killed and three were wounded in action. Col. Howe still limped from a grenade slug.

One of my favorite officers is Maj. David Anderson, who lived in Okemos, near Lansing. Dave is a good officer and a swell fellow. He volunteered to take me up front on the Villa Verde, though the front is everywhere on the flanking mountains overlooking the low few miles of the Villa Verde Trail on the Little Burma Road the combat engineers had built.

We crawled along in a jeep. Dave laughed as we rode. "That hole in the windshield in front of you," he said, "is from a Jap bullet. Fellow sitting there was hit the other day."

It was hard going. The jeep moved over, its rear tires on the edge of the cliff, a dozen times. We crawled high over a landslide on the Little Burma. We passed two bulldozers at work. Finally, the trail was so narrow we got out to hike.

It was the first time I had been off the Little Burma Road. It was the first time I had been on the Villa Verde footpath, the first time ahead of the bulldozers and the engineers.

Before starting out with Dave, I had talked to Corp. Eugene M. Lowe, of Route No. 8, Jackson, while he cleaned his rifle. His communications outfit had laid down 60 miles of telephone wire on the Villa Verde. Others had put down still more.

I had crawled up a steep hill and sat in a foxhole talking to Sergt. Salvatore S. Coruna, of Huntington, Calif. He knew Corp. Jack Glickoff, of the Collingwood Apartments, Detroit, and Pfc. Michael Mikula, of Detroit, both riflemen somewhere in the hills.

"Glick is a regimental runner," Sergt. Coruna said. "He has made a lot of trips to the front under fire. He and Mike are rugged guys."

I was thinking about them as Dave and I walked slowly down the Villa Verde footpath. They were so alive and vital, and here was the rank, pungent smell of death. Jap bodies lay sprawled in sudden death everywhere on the mountain slopes. The Japs never bury their dead.

We passed Yanks carrying litters, with Yank dead, five of them covered by ponchos, carrying them up the steep trail.

I saw my old friend, Warrant Officer Bill Agy, sitting on a

water can, on the hillside, talking on the telephone, in the hot sun. He waved and we stopped to talk.

"Got the Japs licked," Bill said. "Just smashed them to smithereens up here. Our regiment has killed 2,500 Japs and taken 82 Jap machine guns. Good stuff, boy."

We stopped to talk to Pfc. Milford A. Pease, of Williamston, an old friend. He was throwing a big mortar shell into the biggest Yank mortar I had seen. It went off with a terrific roar. "Nice job," he said. He pointed to a captured Jap Juki machine gun.

We walked past Chocolate Drop hill where a Yank lieutenant-colonel, a fine fighting leader, had been killed leading his troops. Finally, we saw the green expanse of the beautiful Cayagan Valley.

Dave pointed to a brown spot on Hill 525, where our Yanks had sneaked in at night with some heavy machine guns, set up, and ambushed 100 Japs at dawn. We looked over 526 where "Easy" Company had attacked at dawn one day, crossing a deep ravine at night, and caught the Japs at breakfast—and wiped them out!

Sitting in some fresh dirt was Pvt. William W. Kilbourn, of Vassar, Mich., driver of a bulldozer.

Firing broke out sharply on the hillside. Another Yank patrol at work. Fr. Rudolph A. Marzion, of Milwaukee, the regiment's chaplain, came walking up from the front lines. He gave us a swig of warm water from his canteen.

Down a steep climb on the trail into a little valley was Corp. George T. Sherwood, 18250 Littlefield avenue, Detroit, sitting on a camp chair with mortars booming above him—getting a GI haircut.

"When you need a haircut, you gotta get it, anywhere," he said. He gave us our first laugh in two hours. Swell fellow, George Sherwood.

Somebody came up another steep turn in the trail. It was

Pfc. William Dymond, of National Mine, Mich., a company runner.

We climbed down a steep hill, very slowly, into a deep gully where the 2nd Battalion was camped in foxholes with poncho covers. Some of the foxholes were deep with rainwater.

Through our field glasses, Maj. Maurice C. Holden, of Cherryvale, Kan., showed us the little red school house of the mountain village of Imugan. That morning the boys of "George" Company had rapped their knuckles on the school house for luck. It had taken 119 days of bitter fighting to get there.

A red flare went up. An answering white flare went up. Elements of the 128th and the 126th Infantry regiments had met out in the hills.

"Your Michigan boys are out there, Carlisle," Maj. Holden said. "Good fighters, those Michigan guys."

We looked at Hill 527, where the last tough Jap opposition was broken, a hill denuded of all vegetation, battle scarred.

More small arms-fire broke out on a wooded hill about 400 yards away, patrol action.

"I thought the campaign was over," I said, naively.

"It is strategically and tactically on the Villa Verde," Maj. Holden said. "But there is always something going on. We just keep cutting the Japs up."

« 40 »

A Dress for a Filipino Girl

UP ON THE VILLA VERDE TRAIL came Miss Wilhelmine Haley, of Norfolk, Neb., a Red Cross worker—the first white woman on the trail in 10 years.

She handed me a letter, a very touching letter, written by a 14-year-old Filipino girl to a woman in Shelby, Mich. It was a letter of gratitude.

Maybe one dress doesn't mean much to the women of Michigan. But in the foothills of the Caraballo Mountains, where the refugees have come, it means so much, so very much, because they have so little.

The Igorots, the hill people, the women and children, have come out of the hills, while their men fight with the division. And these little Igorots, some not five feet in height, make some of the best native warriers in the Philippines.

There are other Filipino refugees, too. Most of their menfolk are carriers for the Red Arrow Division, carrying supplies, food and ammo up to the front lines, where they are on the mountains on the flanks of the Villa Verde and cannot be reached by truck or jeep.

So the Red Cross has been supplying these refugees (these women, young girls and children) with 20,000 articles of clothing sent from the states by Red Cross chapters.

Eight hundred dresses a day are being distributed to 1,500 Filipinos and 5,500 Igorots in San Nicolas, Santa Maria and Natividad—the towns in the foothills in the Red Arrow Division's combat area—under the supervision of Miss Haley.

Some day Miss Marion G. Schultz, of Shelby, Mich., one of the volunteer Red Cross workers—one of the women of America who help the war refugees of the world out of the charity in their souls—will receive this letter of thanks.

I have it before me. It is written in English, in a fine hand that might have been penned by an American girl.

It was written by Miss Magdalena Ramos Tabajunda, of the Natividad High School—Natividad, in Pangasinan Province, the Philippines.

"Miss Schultz," wrote Miss Tabajunda, "I am wishing you are in good health upon receiving my concise missive, and extending you my warmest gratitude. As for me, I am just all right, tackling all hardships.

"My father died in this war on June 17, 1942. I am a daughter of a poor family. My father died on the battlefield. Now I am living with my sister who is married to a poor farmer.

"They have three children and they can't even afford to buy a school dress for me. I help my sister by selling fruits and cakes, by washing American clothes for soldiers.

"Miss Schultz, I am going to tell you the story of the dress which you sent me. One day Mr. Flora, my American history and English teacher, told me to go to our principal teacher's office.

"He showed me the dress and the tag bearing your name. He gave me the dress because he knew my poor situation.

"Miss Schultz, how can I ever repay you? Now I am in the first year, I am studying in the Natividad High School. Even though we are very poor my sister sent me to school. I am not ashamed to wear old clothes, which are darned, so long as they are clean ones.

"So I thank you, Miss Schultz for your nice dress. I can remodel it and I can wear it to school. To tell you the truth, Miss Schultz, I sometimes cannot concentrate my mind on my lessons because of my poor life and too much work, and lack of clothes to wear.

"Now you have sent me a new and durable dress.

"How can I thank you and repay you, Miss Schultz?

"Thanks a million, Miss Schultz. May God bless you, always."

So that was the letter of this 14-year-old Filipino girl whose father died and fought on our side, to Miss Schultz.

And the soldiers of the 32nd Division, at whose side the Filipino and the Igorot men are fighting on the Villa Verde trail, thank you, too, Miss Schultz.

« 41 »

90 Pounds of Misery

ALMOST EVERYTHING happened that day.

In the early morning two gleaming Mustangs came over our camp on the mountainside and buzzed the camp at 20 feet at an angle that made your hair stand up. They dove and circled.

"What's going on?" I asked Lieut.-Col. George A. Bond, Jr., a busy officer in the Red Arrow Division.

"I sent the pilots some Jap souvenirs yesterday," he said, smiling, as he watched the Mustangs. "They've just come over to thank us. Great bunch of fellows, those pilots."

I spent 11 hours up on the Villa Verde that day, freezing to death at 6 a. m., feeling like a fried chicken at noon in the hot sun, and sloshing through the mud and rain in the late afternoon.

What a day that was!

The division broke the back of the Jap resistance on the trail. The Thunderbolts dive-bombed their new positions. One of our patrols caught some Japs trying to make a sneak attack about 500 yards from me.

I was an unwilling spectator to some hot, fast action across the draw. Through my field glasses I saw how well our boys shoot.

Down the trail that day a two-and-a-half ton truck poked lazily around the hairpin turns. It was full of captured Jap grenades and artillery shells and mortars. It was, of course, a bumpy ride. Suddenly the whole shebang went off, like a Fourth of July celebration. The driver and his guard jumped to safety, with a few minor burns.

I talked to them for a moment—lads from Arkansas and Pennsylvania.

"Cripes!" said the driver, "I've driven all through this campaign under all sorts of fire and never got a scratch. And then I am driving along, thinking about my baby girl, and—Bang! Bang! Plop! Boom!—the whole works let loose."

To see and talk to troops you have to crawl up steep slopes and sit in muddy foxholes. I was exhausted when I got back.

At 11 p.m., some muddy but rugged GI riflemen brought in a Jap prisoner, a very Sad Sack. They sat him down in the corner of a tent and gave him a couple of cigarets out of a K ration.

"T'ank you, sirrrrh," he said.

I asked Col. Bond if I could talk to this Nip.

"If he'll talk to you, you may," he said. "But you can't ask him any questions of a military nature."

Well, I wasn't much interested in Jap tactics, because the 32nd Division had made Jap tactics seem ridiculous, anyway. So into the tent I went.

A big, tough MP with a carbine across his knee was guarding the prisoner. The MP was about 6 feet 5, weighing at least 220; one of those men from the hills of Tennessee who make fine soldiers.

The Jap soldier was 5 feet tall and weighed about 90 pounds. The Yank was strong, husky, rugged, well-fed, happy. The Jap was small, underfed, undernourished, a poor specimen of a soldier. But soldiers in defeat always have that hangdog air of silent desperation.

The Jap was barefooted, his feet muddy and badly swollen, with large, open sores. He was wearing a private's muddy raincoat over his filthy uniform. He scratched himself continually. There were sores over his body. He needed a haircut, and grime was caked on his face.

He said he had not eaten in five days. He had beri-beri. His platoon had left him alone on a hill because he was sick.

Our Yanks are different. They carry the sick and the wounded back to our lines, under fire, down cliffs.

I asked this Jap if he didn't think it was a dirty trick to be deserted by his own outfit.

"We had . . . an order . . . order is order . . . move out. That is order."

He said he was "the miserable one," and he looked it. He told me his superior private, a rank higher, had been beating him up.

He knew Tokyo was being bombed (his home is near it) and he made a sad face. It amazed me that he conceded that the Japs were losing the Villa Verde campaign. I asked him why he thought so.

"We retreat . . . retreat . . . retreat . . . so much," he said. He spoke in a low voice. Sometimes he was hard to understand.

He had a scrawny mustache and a scrawny, tiny beard.

He felt that it was very dishonorable to retreat. But up on Hill 527 he had given up. He threw away his shoes. He threw away his pack. He threw away his rifle. He was trying to stumble into his own lines when a Yank patrol caught him.

I asked him what he thought was going to happen to him. He said he expected to be killed. An American officer explained to him patiently that he would not.

The Jap sucked on the butt of a cigaret.

"Me," he said slowly, "me . . . miserable one."

« 42 »

The Colonel Was a School Teacher

THE FORMER GRAND RAPIDS high school teacher was not sitting in his own sandbag-quarters in the gully in the mountains off the Villa Verde.

A Jap shell had landed on the slope above his dugout, caving a small landslide into the quarters of Col. Merle H. Howe, commander of the 128th Infantry Regiment, former history, science and math teacher at Union High School in Grand Rapids.

"The Japs had these hills dug out like a prairie dog town," Col. Howe said. "Our boys had to dig them out or seal them up. I always get a kick out of hearing one of my officers say to one of his men, 'Hey, Joe, take a pole charge and blow out that Nip hole.'"

When the 32nd first started fighting on the Villa Verde, each company had an assault team. After 120 days of fighting the Jap in the mountains, almost every rifleman was a one-man assault team!

That means that every GI had learned how to handle a demolition charge—a pole charge or a hand charge!

Col. Howe is a front-line leader. When I last saw him he was still limping around the front lines with a Jap hand-grenade slug in his right leg. He refused to go to the rear.

"Some day," he said, "I'll have that piece of shell cut out."

Here is Col. Howe's story of the fighting on the Villa Verde:

"The Japs were experts at defensive fighting in the mountains," he explained. "In the draws we found two holes covering a trail. But another hidden hole would conceal a machine gun. It would cut loose at our boys.

"But our GI's learn quickly. What makes the American soldier the best fighting man in the world is the fact that he can readily adapt himself to anything new.

"Our boys learned to find the blind spots to the caves. If four caves were protecting each other, the GIs would knock off a cave on the flank. This made a blind spot on the next one.

"I was following a patrol one day. The last man went wide on the curve. A Nip stood up and fired at him. He started after him, and found six adjoining holes full of Nips. That's the way the fighting went. We found often that the trail side of the caves was too tough. Our boys had to circle and crack 'em from the rear of the cave. Hard work. Tough climbing. But successful!

"I'm a bit proud of our regiment. We cracked Salacsac Pass, and Hill 508 (the Japs called it Kongo) and Hill 505 (the Japs called it Mt. Tenno). They commanded everything on the Villa Verde. But my boys cracked them!"

Col. Howe paused a moment to open a message from a battalion commander up ahead on the trail, reached for the phone. Later he resumed his story.

"Take Hill 505," he continued. "We cracked it by digging. On our perimeter, the Japs were shooting 35 yards away at us with machine guns. We dug a tunnel only three feet deep, a mere slit trench really. We had to go 35 yards to the Nip positions; they were on the crest of the slope.

"Our boys dug with trenching tools, with sandbags in front of them as they dug, pushing the sandbags along with the Jap machine guns chewing at the bags.

"We got one of our machine guns in the slit trench at night. The next day the Nip machine guns cut loose. Our men would duck, raise up, cut loose with ours. In one hour we knocked out their main machine gun.

"Our boys set off a pole charge when we got up to the Nip positions, blew them to hell. We found one of our armored-piercing machine gun bullets wedged down the barrel of the Nip machine gun. That's shooting, brother!

"Weird things happened. Some nights our men on the top of a hill couldn't sleep since the Nips were digging like the devil on the hillside below them!

"We kept gnawing away at the Nips. We finally broke them. Our people began to hear explosions in the earth under them. The despondent Nips were blowing themselves up with their own hand grenades.

"One of our machine guns had been firing from a position for four or five days. One day the Japs came digging out of a hole near it."

Howe laughed and said to Maj. Dave Anderson, of Lansing, "Hey, Andy, remember that tug of war?"

"Sure do," said Andy.

"Well," said Col. Howe, "one night in the moonlight a Yank in his foxhole on a slope looked down. He saw a Jap machine gun poking its nose out of a cave we thought was sealed. Poking its barrel through the dirt. A lot of our troops were below it.

"GI's are wonderful! This GI reached down with his Garand and hooked on to the Jap machine gun barrel with his rifle. He pulled. The Jap pulled. For a few minutes it was a tug of war. The GI fired eight shots. The Jap let go. The GI got him the next morning.

"'George' Company had positions the size of a postage stamp on Hill 506, with the Japs all around. Sent a combat patrol up there to help the company out. They started digging in, discovered a big Jap cave right in the middle of our defense perimeter, blasted the cave with demolition charges.

"But the Japs are unpredictable. At 3 a. m. five Japs dug their way out of the sealed cave. A Nip officer with a saber in both hands rushed a GI. The GI's carbine jammed.

"He grabbed the saber with his hands. The Jap pulled away, slashing at the GI. The saber hit our rifleman's helmet, knocked it down on his face, blacked both his eyes. But the lad was game! He grabbed the Jap saber with his hands, took it away from the officer, and killed him. We polished off the rest of the Nips.

"Take Hill 505. Our boys were digging in, making a perimeter defense on the crest of the hill. The Japs were digging in on the other side of the hill.

"Some of our boys caved in on them, dropping 10 feet into the Jap cave. That's how they wiped out the Japs—fell right into them."

Now you know, from the words of Col. Howe, how tough, how violent the Villa Verde campaign was.

But our boys won it!

« 43 »

The General Waits for the Private

IT ISN'T EVERY DAY that a private first class keeps a two-star General waiting for two hours. But Maj.-Gen. W. H. Gill, commander of the Red Arrow Division, is a friend of the GI's and he understood. He wasn't the least bit put out.

For Pfc. Harold V. Matthews, 136 Clairmount street, Detroit, really couldn't help it. He came out of the front lines, the traffic was tough on the Villa Verde, and he did the best he could.

Gen. Gill was waiting to decorate Pfc. Matthews with the Silver Star for gallantry in action, along with three other Detroit veterans. The General waited two hours. He could not wait any longer. He wanted to get up to the front, himself.

But Matthews got his Silver Star.

"My gosh," he said, "I hope the General isn't mad at me."

Headquarters staff officers assured him the General was not angry.

Matthews was carrying a battle-scarred rifle when I saw him. A few nights before he was in his foxhole on the Villa Verde. The Japs poured mortars into his area. A piece of shrapnel hit in his hole. His carbine was at his elbow, standing upright. Shrapnel hit it, exploding the bullet in the carbine's chamber.

"I thought I was hit—for a moment," Matthews said.

Matthews sat down in the grass on the hillside.

"Wouldn't that have been something?" he asked. "Shot by my own carbine!"

Matthews received his Silver Star for participating in a sharp action, in which he was wounded. He has since recovered and is fit and none the worse for his experience.

It was hard work getting the story out of him. GI's don't like to talk about their exploits. They get under fire. They meet the Jap at 20 feet, as Matthews did, and then they do things that surprise themselves, as Matthews was surprised.

A soldier never knows what he will do in a tight spot. He is trained well. He learns from experience. He is well led by his officers. And then—without warning—comes the spontaneity of action where the decisions, what he does, how he fights, all those things, are up to him alone.

For fighting is a personal thing to a GI. It has all the devastating closeness of a one-man show. Others feel the same thing, many others, but for the GI, like Matthews, it is his very own fight.

Now you take Pfc. Matthews. He was the second scout on a small patrol that crept out 2,000 yards beyond our lines in the mountains, crept up to the lower edge of a steep ridge, looking for stray Japs, looking for pockets of them.

There were just 20 soldiers in that patrol, and nothing tries the daring, the ingenuity and the alertness of fighting men more than these patrols.

The first scout, alert as he was, passed up some Japs hidden in the tall kunai grass. Matthews spotted a Jap crawling along the ridge with a hand grenade in his hand.

Matthews could see only about four inches of the Jap's back.

But the Army had taught Matthews how to shoot. He opened fire. The Jap spun around, fell down, with a bullet between his shoulder blades.

The Detroit private moved forward. Other hidden Japs fired at him.

"I heard a rifle shot." Matthews said. "It hit my helmet. It nicked me on the side of the head. The bullet cut into my shoulder and came out my arm. I knew I was hit. My helmet flew off. I fell down."

And then what happened?

Matthews is still a little vague about that except that he became fighting mad, with a flaming GI hatred that is the backbone of the American Army.

Consider the 32nd Division's official citation about Matthews.

"In spite of injury," it read, "Pfc. Matthews charged the enemy, firing as he advanced and inflicting other casualties."

What a guy!

"The patrol rallied," the citation read, "and killed the enemy."

When the action was over, a medical aid man took care of Matthews.

Matthews took his Silver Star out of its case, while we talked, looking at it, quietly, just staring.

"Pretty little gadget," he said. "I never thought I could win one."

« 44 »

Your Boy Died a Hero

THIS IS AN OPEN letter to a Michigan mother whose only son was killed on the Villa Verde Trail in the Caraballo Mountains with the Red Arrow Division.

Mrs. Olive Burgess, 99 Hamilton court, Pontiac, wrote your Detroit News war correspondent that her only son, Pfc. Earl F. Burgess, with the Medical Detachment of the 126th Infantry, had died of wounds on Luzon April 11.

"Earl was all I had," she said. "All I had. It would help so much in bearing this if I only knew what happened. What was he doing? How did my boy die?"

Mrs. Burgess, the fighting veterans of the 126th Regiment called your son "P-38." You know what P-38 is, Mrs. Burgess? One of the finest fighter planes in the world today. Our fighter plane.

Of course, you will want to know why these infantrymen called your boy that. Pfc. Howard Lewis of Greenville, South Carolina, a medical aid man with the 126th, knew the answer.

For Pfc. Lewis knew your son so well. They were pals. They shipped to the Southwest Pacific together; they became close friends at Saidor. They worked together saving the lives of front-line soldiers who were wounded in action at Yakamul, near Aitape, in New Guinea, and on Luzon.

When the going was tough, Pfc. Lewis said old "P-38" Burgess had a lot of stuff on the ball. He was a litter bearer with the front-line troops. He was the fastest man we had in getting to a wounded man. He feared nothing. He just went up there and got him out.

The speed with which he did that won a lot of admiration in

our regiment. You know how fast the P-38 fighter is? The fastest thing there is in the air. So the boys of the regiment started calling him P-38.

And, Mrs. Burgess, did a boy so far from home ever win a finer nickname? For fighting soldiers are like that. They pin a nickname on everyone. But this time it was more than a nickname. It was a laurel of respect.

And today when we watched a flight of P-38's flying over the Red Arrow Division, Pfc. Albert J. Jones, of 60 Florida avenue, West Youngstown, O., remarked: "Every time I see them I think of 'P-38' Burgess."

In those words of a GI with the 32nd, Mrs. Burgess, you will feel the touch of immortality your boy has won in the memories of so many of the lads of the Red Arrow who knew him.

"P-38 Burgess," said Pfc. Jones, "was a quiet fellow. He was friends with everybody. He was one of the best liked boys in the whole regiment.

"There was a reason for that. No matter what was asked of him he did it. Always on the job. He was slight in build, you know, but he never complained when he carried litter after litter of wounded men up and down muddy mountain trails. So often under fire.

"I sure got a kick out of 'P-38' in action. When it was really hot up there and the Nips were throwing everything at us, he would always say: 'Well, I got to get out there and bring in one more man.'

"It was always one more man with him until all the wounded were safely in, all being tended to at the battalion aid station."

That was the kind of a soldier your boy was, Mrs. Burgess.

You want to know what happened to him, Mrs. Burgess, and these are the facts as given to me by Red Arrow men who were with him that day.

There is considerable consolation for you in these facts. Your boy was out trying to save the life of another Red Arrow veteran, a wounded rifleman, when he himself was hit.

These are the facts: At 1300 hours (1 p. m.) in the Mt. Imugan area of the Villa Verde Trail your son left the 1st Battalion aid station with three medics and two other men.

Their names: Pfc. Odell Beatty, Box 212, Clayton, Ala., and Pfc. George Sloyka, Box 38, Colner, Pa., both of the Ammunition and Pioneer Platoon. Also Pfc. Donald Greenwood, Ashley, Ind.; Sergt. Malcolm E. Larrow, RFD 1, LaSalle, Mich., and Pfc. Edwin Ray, 4018 Garrow street, Houston, Tex.

They started out for C Company, your son and these others. They had to crawl across an open area. Long-range Jap machine guns opened up on them. But they got to the company safely.

A wounded soldier was lying out in front of the company's perimeter of defense, lying there alone in need of medical attention. Your son, Mrs. Burgess, and these others volunteered to go out and bring him into our lines.

Your son and his five companions were under direct enemy observation from close-up range as they started out. They reached the wounded veteran. The medical aid men gave him first aid. They stopped the flow of blood with tourniquets. They gave him a shot of morphine.

They started to bring him in in a litter your boy carried out there, Mrs. Burgess.

Your son was carrying one side of the rear end of the wounded rifleman's stretcher. As they carried him slowly back, the Japs opened up on this little group of lifesavers with mortars.

A 90 mm. Jap mortar shell landed three yards behind them. The wounded man on the litter was killed instantly. All six, including your son, were wounded.

The riflemen of C Company did not let your son lie out

there in No Man's Land, Mrs. Burgess. As they stormed out of their perimeter, some of them blasted the hidden Japs with machine guns. Others carried your son out. Still others carried his companions into our lines.

All the fast efficient medical machinery of the regiment went into operation to save your son and those five others. Sloyka, Greenwood, Larrow and Ray recovered, were awarded Purple Hearts and have since returned from a field hospital to duty. Beatty was seriously wounded. He is now convalescing in a hospital in the States.

Your son, Mrs. Burgess, because of his position at the litter nearest to the mortar shell, was the most seriously wounded. Yet, again, there is some consolation for you. He never knew what hit him. He was knocked unconscious. He never recovered consciousness. He died so soon after being wounded that it could almost be said he was killed in action. But the Army is precise. He is listed as having died of wounds from mortar fragments.

You may take some pride, too, Mrs. Burgess, in your son's soldier rating—superior; character rating, excellent.

He is buried today at the USAF Cemetery No. 1 at Santa Barbara, Luzon. It is a beautiful cemetery, Mrs. Burgess, with tall stately palm trees, with white crosses on the graves from the chestnut trees of America and with grass and flowers from back home on those graves.

You will want to know, too, about how so many of the Red Arrow boys made the long trek to the cemetery by jeep, by truck, by hitchhiking down the Villa Verde Trail, to say a last farewell to your son at his grave.

And I thought it so spendid that almost to a man all the veterans of C Company, the soldiers who were with him when he was killed, all those veterans made that pilgrimage.

So now you have the story of your son's death, Mrs. Burgess. In the shroud of your grief at losing your only son you know

now how much the boys of the 126th, a great fighting regiment, respected and admired him.

Perhaps Pfc. Lewis wrote your son's epitaph.

"All of us liked old 'P-38' Burgess," he said. "He saved so many lives."

El Lobo Means the Wolf

« 45 »

YOU NEVER KNOW what our Army and the enemy will do to a soldier. Some of the best fighting men in the Red Arrow Division would never be cast for their unusual roles by the Hollywood casting directors.

Somehow, by some magic of metamorphosis, the quiet fellow or the noisy chap you knew back home develops into a great fighting man. Somewhere along the line of fighting experience the war took him over and changed his personality, his way of life, his thought processes.

The 128th Infantry Regiment of the 32nd, commanded by that fighting leader Col. Merle H. Howe, of Grand Rapids, did a terrific amount of campaigning in the mountains. It was the backbone of the successful finish fight that won the campaign.

So many officers and so many GI's have done startling things for the 128th. But the regiment thinks of Lieut. Charles T. R. Bohannan, of Washington, D. C., in legendary terms.

While I was up at the front with the regiment, many a Detroit GI asked me: "Hey, Jack, have you met Old Lobo yet?"

I talked to them about him in their hillside foxholes, or as they scrambled along the Villa Verde. I checked their stories with Col. Howe and my hiking companion, Maj. Dave Anderson, of Lansing. Andy had a lot of lore on El Lobo.

What amazed me most was that Lieut. Bohannan—the El Lobo of GI legend—was an archaeologist for the Smithsonian Institute of Washington.

Now he is the leader of a long-range recon platoon for the 128th, a platoon that is always creeping into the Jap lines, sometimes for weeks at a time, and raising hob with the Jap communications, supplies and morale.

The stories about Lobo are endless. Yet one of them, a more recent one, illustrates his fighting temper. For Col. Howe told me that Bohannan had "just plain, unadulterated guts!" up on the Villa Verde.

Consider this action:

The Lobo platoon came out of the Jap lines and took up its so-called "rest area" with a front-line infantry company, bivouacking in abandoned Jap caves on the mountainside.

The Japs had a trail block on the Villa Verde up ahead, 20 Japs with a light machine gun, Jap tommyguns, hand grenades, satchels of TNT and rifles. Very well equipped, those Nips.

This trail block was a lot of trouble for our troops, putting them under constant fire.

"I'm going to clean those buzzards out," Lobo said, though "buzzard" is a euphemism for a more violent GI term for the enemy.

Lobo took six of his men with him, crawled up close to the Jap positions, scouted out their positions. Then they crawled back and collected two squads of riflemen. Lobo had found the Japs were holed up in eight caves over, under and on the sides of the Villa Verde.

With the 24 men in the squads and his own six scouts, Lobo attacked. This gallant officer crawled alone into a Jap cave, and came running out like a sprinter.

There was an explosion behind him. He wheeled around, rushed back into the cave. His men saw him wrestling with a

Jap officer in the cave. With his old-style Colt .45, Lobo killed the Jap.

"Old Betsy failed me just once," he said. "I ran into that Jap the first time. I pulled the trigger. My pistol misfired. First time it happened. The Jap threw a hand grenade at me."

With leadership like that, the squads went to work. Lobo led the attacks on cave after cave. His men killed 18 Japs at point-blank range and buried 25 others with demolition charges.

What type of an officer is this Lobo? Well, he is a tall, thin, red-headed lieutenant who once spent a month within the Jap lines in the Leyte campaign. Like so many individualists, he is on the eccentric side. Other officers have to hunt him down to get five pesos ($2.50) a week out of him for the officers' mess.

Yet he gave a Filipino guerilla a wrist watch costing 50 pesos ($25)!

He hung his nickname on himself. In his radio communications with our lines, while out on patrol in the enemy lines, the radio operators always fumbled with his name.

"Dammit," he said one day, "just call me Lobo. My name was never intended for a radio pin-up boy!"

So Lobo the legendary he became!

« 46 »

A Gallant Captain Lives in Memory

THE RED ARROWS missed Capt. Herman Bottcher on the Villa Verde Trail.

Capt. Bottcher was killed in Leyte by a Jap artillery shell, while leading the cavalry recon troop far behind the enemy lines.

Still, at night in their foxholes during the Villa Verde campaign the infantry riflemen talked about Capt. Bottcher. For to the recon troop, again out in the Jap lines without him, his memory was fresh and vivid and inspiring.

You must have heard of Capt. Bottcher. He was one of the most magnificent soldiers in the Southwest Pacific. Officers of the 6th Army avow that he was one of the greatest soldiers of World War II.

But better than all his acclaim, all his military genius, the fighting men of the 32nd Division loved him.

The entire division hit the Japs in uncontrollable fury after Capt. Bottcher's death.

Naturally, there are many great commanders and many rugged fighting men in a division such as this. Yet the most spectacular was Capt. Bottcher.

He came up from the ranks from private to captain and would have gone still further had he lived.

Capt. Bottcher led the breakthrough at Buna, in New Guinea, with only a platoon of 31 men. There are three left of that platoon now, all former Michigan National Guardsmen.

Staff Sergt. Melvin Babcock and Sergt. Gordon Blum, both of Stanton, and Staff Sergt. Roland G. Acheson, 519 Monroe street, Lowell, Mich., probably know more about Capt. Bottcher than any other men in the division.

Corp. Warren W. Blodgett, of Grand Rapids, was standing beside Bottcher when he was hit and caught him in his arms.

Blodge still wipes away the tears when he talks of the captain's death.

Blum said: "He was strictly a man's man, a private at heart."

Babcock: "He was a nervous type of guy. He always had to be doing something."

Blum: "But he would ask you to do something in a way that made you want to do it."

Babcock: "He would never lead you in blind."

Acheson: "He explained things simply and well to the men. He always tried to give you the whole picture."

They have memories of Bottcher that are typical GI memories.

Bottcher never ducked at small arm's fire. "After you hear it crack," he explained, "it's too late to duck!"

In the Buna fight, the entire Yank force was held up by intense Jap fire. Bottcher called for volunteers to crack the Japs. His entire platoon of 31 volunteered.

Bottcher took the lead.

They crawled through waist-high swamp water. Sniper bullets kicked around. The Jap artillery hammered them. Suddenly Bottcher dove under water! A shell landed a few feet from him, stunned him, broke an ear drum. On he went.

Bottcher's men hugged the jungle to the beach's edge.

His men cut down the Japs from the flank. Bottcher crawled out under fire and brought a wounded GI in.

Bottcher unerringly picked a position that cut the village from the mission area, by putting his platoon between a maze of Jap tunnels and pillbox positions.

His men had driven a wedge into the Jap pool of supplies and troops. It was the first time the Jap lines had been pierced in that campaign. The division moved up in support of Bottcher's small force, and the Battle of Buna was won.

Bottcher was wounded four times at Buna, and led the final attack on the Buna Triangle with his left arm in a sling!

So now you know to some extent why the fighting men of the 32nd loved this gallant captain so.

Capt. Bottcher is dead, but he still lives for all time in the memory of the Red Arrow Division. It is an immortality of memory that few soldiers achieve.

« 47 »

The Price of Successful War

THIS STORY deals with the death and burial of some of America's finest, who were cut down in youth by enemy bullets and shells.

It deals with the extreme price of successful war.

Though it is somewhat grim, it will show the folks back home how the 32nd Division and other divisions of the gallant 6th Army—give a last fitting tribute to their dead.

For no Yank soldier in Northern Luzon who is killed in action or dies of his wounds is buried in a nameless grave!

I visited the cemetery of the United States Armed Forces, Santa Barbara No. I, today. I didn't feel like making the trip, for purely selfish personal reasons. Every man in uniform likes to pull the blinds down on the thought of death at the front. It is always present. You just try to forget about it.

So I set out to find the answers to questions in the minds of all the folks back home who have lost sons and brothers, husbands and sweethearts in Northern Luzon.

Santa Barbara No. I is a beautiful cemetery, with the American flag flying in the three terraces of a center drive, with stone flaggings and terraces of hedges and flowers.

Under rows of palm trees, there stretched seven acres of the graves of American dead.

Many GI's and officers of the Red Arrow Division are buried here. There are several thousand Yanks at rest in the cemetery.

Here lie the men of the 32nd. Of the 33rd, the 37th and the 25th who all fought on the flanks of the Red Arrow in the current campaign. Men of the 43rd and the 6th divisions; the Air Forces, the Navy and the Marine Corps.

Bodies are brought in by truck to a collecting station. Sometimes they are rewrapped there. There a tally sheet is made of each dead soldier, giving his rank, name, serial number, and date of death and his organization. Every precaution is taken so that every body is identified.

The bodies are taken to the Santa Barbara Cemetery by truck. They seldom arrive alone.

It is amazing how much loyalty men of platoons and companies and regiments show to their dead pals.

Each body is registered again, with forms in triplicate that record the name, rank, serial number, organization, time and date of burial, grave number and row number, and what soldiers are buried on each side.

Lieut. Steve W. Mason, of New Mexico, is the commander of the cemetery. Sergt. Howard A. Wilson, of Middletown, O., a former Presbyterian missionary in the Far East, said that eight Army personnel supervise the cemetery, employing 350 Filipino workers.

The bodies are embalmed in the morgue. The soldier's "dog tags" are divided into two sections. One is placed around his neck. If his tags are lost, a report is placed in a container in his casket.

The Yanks are buried in blue gray caskets made in Australia. Each has a military funeral.

The chaplains come down from their regiments, or from the Air Forces. Services are held on the terraces, with an American flag draped over the coffin, and the flag at half staff. Every soldier gets a funeral service of his own religion by a chaplain of his religion.

I walked out through the long rows of white crosses. Hewn from the chestnut trees of America and shipped here.

Sergt. Wilson pointed out the graves of three Detroiters, names he had chosen at random.

We took off our caps before the grave of Pfc. Edward Schedlo, of 5145 Argyle, Dearborn, killed in action April 18.

Of Pfc. Anthony Tavolaggi, an infantryman, 61 Longwood east, Detroit, killed in action April 8.

Of Pfc. Edward A. Harsewski, an infantryman, killed in action Feb. 18.

Tall palm trees shaded their graves.

Newly planted grass was growing on them. Over in the cemetery's greenhouse, the batchelor buttons and the verbenas of America were growing, ready to be transplanted to the graves.

Well, these Detroit boys were so far from home and the folks they loved—10,600 miles.

There are times when a man is not ashamed of his tears.

« 48 »

Gill's Boys Get the Best

IN A SPECIAL message of assurance to Detroit relatives of soldiers fighting with the 32nd Division, Maj.-Gen. W. H. Gill, commander of the Red Arrow Division, declared that "when your soldier has been wounded in action he gets the very best medical treatment possible."

Well aware that relatives always worry when their soldiers are wounded in action (and Gen. Gill's son was wounded in action in Germany with the Yank forces)—Gen. Gill made an exclusive recording here for Radio Station WWJ-The Detroit News, which was broadcast last night.

"I know you worry," Gen. Gill said, addressing the fathers, the mothers, the wives and all the relatives of Detroit soldiers in his division, veterans of the Villa Verde Trail operation.

"And I want you to know that when your boy is wounded we take good care of him.

"Your boy has trained with us, fought with us. When the Jap shrapnel or bullets cut him down, then life-saving plans begin to operate.

"Our medical organization includes some of the finest and most experienced surgeons in civilian life. Their job is to save your boy's life, and they are very successful. Recently, I looked over the list of one of our regiments. Of the wounded — 98½ per cent were saved!"

Gen. Gill took a hypothetical case, so that every relative of Red Arrow men would know precisely what happens.

"The operation on the Villa Verde Trail put this system to its greatest test," Gen. Gill said. "Let's assume that your son, Willie Brown, is wounded in action.

"At 10:15 the morning of May 12, Brown was hit by shell fragments in the upper arm and chest. The company aid man crawls to his side, rips away clothing, examines the wound and applies a dressing.

"Because of the seriousness of the wound, the aid man gives Brown a shot of morphine, makes him as comfortable as possible until the litter bearers arrive to move him back to the battalion aid station.

"In our recent mountain fighting we have found that as many as 12 men were needed to evacuate a single wounded man.

"Upon arriving at the aid station 30 minutes later, at 10:45 a. m., the battalion surgeon examines Brown's wounds. Here plasma is given, counteracting shock, and strengthening him to withstand the journey to the portable surgical hospital. Here, too, splints are applied to the arm, and the dressings removed and changed where necessary.

"Brown is made as comfortable as possible," Gen. Gill said, "and placed in an ambulance."

"He is carried by ambulance," Gill added, "over eight miles of rough, tortuous mountain roads, to the portable surgical hospital. He is rushed into the operating tent and given an anesthetic. The surgeon removes the shell fragments from his chest, performs other necessary surgery and dresses the wounds. The arm is placed in a cast.

"Brown has lost much blood. It is found necessary to give him a transfusion. Here the miracle of modern medicine appears.

"Human blood—from thousands of volunteer blood donors throughout the United States and flown here in ice containers —is placed in his veins.

"Now recovery begins. Brown is kept in the portable hospital about two days. Then he is moved to the larger, safer hospital in the rear.

"When he is strong enough to be moved again, Brown is flown by L-5—those super Piper Cubs (and 70 of them are in this theater, provided by the school children of Detroit through their war bond savings)—to a field hospital. The trip eliminates a ride by ambulance over rough, bumpy roads of the Philippines."

« 49 »

Memo of a Red Cross Girl

THERE WERE ALWAYS unpleasant and sometimes terrible incidents in the internment camp for 500 Americans at Baguio.

Internees tried so pitifully to avoid these incidents during those three uncertain years. But Jap guards—with their capacity for torture on the helpless—instigated these incidents as often as possible.

Bitter memories of her three years and one month as a Jap prisoner come to Miss Cordelia C. Job, of Saugatuck, Mich.

Now a Red Cross worker in Manila, Miss Job was a teacher at the Brent school in Baguio for American children, when the Japs invaded. By that time most of the 200 children were on their way back to the States.

"Baguio was declared an open city," she said. "The Japs were coming in. So all the American civilians concentrated at the Brent school. We waited.

"They put us at a former American Army post near Baguio. We were assigned to barracks where Igorots had lived.

"They put 500 in one building with room for 100. It was very uncomfortable. Finally, after six months, they took us to another camp, once occupied by the Philippines Constabulary, about six miles from Baguio."

Then the Jap guards started on a studied plan to give them a chance to punish the internees.

"These incidents happened every day," Miss Job said. "We did everything we could to avoid them. But they kept making up new rules. Some of them had no rhyme or reason.

"The Jap guards had a mania for making us women internees bow to them. They were always criticizing our bows. They kept making us bow lower and lower."

Then the internment camp was thrown into turmoil for months by the Jap guards.

"We were getting news from the world outside by radio," Miss Job said. "It annoyed the Japs so much. They were furious because we knew how the Yanks were beating them in the field. They took some of the men to the military police headquarters and tortured them for hours.

"But the boys never told. The Japs knocked them senseless. Yet they never found out we had a radio or where we got it.

"One night two of the Americans went over the wall, escaped, and fought with the guerillas. The Jap guards became violent. From then on they made our lives miserable."

Miss Job was transferred to Bilibid prison in Manila the

last month of her internment. She and a group of American women began making an American flag.

"We hoisted our flag," Miss Job said, "as our American soldiers came into our camp. And then we just cried our eyes out, we were so happy. It was just wonderful—so wonderful—to see our American boys again. They looked so fine."

« 50 »

Red Cross Sparks Morale

THE WOUNDED YANK soldier at the big 60th General Hospital in Manila, though still confined to his bed by injuries, likes fun and laughter.

He likes to play crazy little games, thought up on the spur of the moment by Red Cross Worker Bobbie Rosier, 62 Connecticut avenue, Highland Park, Mich., who does hospital recreation work.

Some of the games are just "kid games," which he hadn't tried since he was a small boy, but he likes them since they bring laughter and memories of home, America, and the boy he once was.

"These wounded soldiers are wonderful—absolutely wonderful," Miss Rosier said. "Actually they are a bunch of kidding guys who like to lie back on their hospital beds and laugh at the other fellow who is trying to amuse himself.

"The wounded boys just do little things. Yet they get such a kick out of them. For example, we have auctions in a ward. We use the 'money' from a Monopoly game. We get up prizes, wrapped and secret, and the boys bid for them and try to figure out what's in the surprise package.

"We put gum and cigarets in those prizes. And if I can find any hair tonic—well, the boy who wins the auction for it is just out of this world!

"We play crazy games, kid games, and we have our own quiz programs. In all of the wards we have bingo tournaments. The boys like to play Chinese checkers, and they are good at it, too. I play a few games with the patients until I get games started between patients in adjoining beds. They play cards and checkers.

"I take craft work into them too. Mostly belt making and leather work, but they enjoy it very much.

"We have a craft shop for our ambulatory patients. They make belts, clogged shoes for shower bath wear, leather goods, chains for 'dog tags.' They also make beautiful leather picture frames.

"We have a recreation hall for these patients who can get around with ping pong tables, card tables and writing desks."

I visited this recreation hall with Miss Rosier. It is a big, roomy place, filled with wounded Yanks in their pajamas. There was a doubles game of ping pong, three Chinese checkers and two checker games, and a card game in action. Somebody played the piano. Some of the boys were writing letters home. There was a big bulletin board filled with the latest cartoons from home.

"What impresses me so much about our Yank wounded is that they ask so little, are contented with so little, and don't lie around feeling sorry for themselves," Miss Rosier said. "They just grin and bear everything.

"Some of them have seen a lot of war. Some of them have spent so many days in front-line fox holes. But in their hospital ward they are just a bunch of fun-loving American fellows who are such really great guys."

« 51 »

Nurses Often Write For Them

THE ONLY GIRL back home should always be proud of the letters she gets from her wounded soldier.

For, in the judgment of Miss Mildred De Long, 706 Hazelwood avenue, Detroit, a former teacher at the Durfee Intermediate School in Detroit and now a Red Cross recreation worker in the 49th General Hospital, the wounded boys "dictate beautiful letters" to women waiting back home for them.

Miss De Long has written thousands of these letters, while wounded Yanks, some of them hardly able to move, some of them speaking in whispers from pain, dictate their letters of love.

"I have written so many of these letters," she said, "that sometimes I think I must have written enough to fill a book shelf. But they are priceless letters. And I have mailed so many Purple Hearts from the boys to their girls.

"These wounded boys put the American girl—their girls—on such high pedestals that I always hope those girls deserve all that.

"It is really marvelous the way these boys just have to get a letter off to their girls, even if they are unable to write them. They are so proud of their girls."

Well I had to ask it.

"Is there any love in those dictated letters?"

"Ah, yes," replied Miss De Long. "Plenty of it. Our boys are not bashful, even while they are dictating a letter through me, about telling their girls how much they love them.

"Why there was one wounded lad, so young, so handsome, so brave, who dictated a letter to his sweetheart. And then he asked me to print across the top of the first page of his letter the words, 'I love you. I love you. I love you.'

"And then, he said to me, 'I always print that on that page of every letter I write to her.'

"As I printed those words, as he asked me, he watched me and smiled. 'She'll understand,' he said. 'It's our own secret code.'

"And those boys worry so much.

"They don't want their girls to worry about them. They always minimize the seriousness of their wounds. And some of them are just sweet fibbers. Today I took dictated letters from three boys with head wounds. Serious wounds. The doctors said they would pull through. And what do you think they all wrote home to the Little Woman?

"They all said, 'Don't worry, Honey. I got hit but it's nothing to worry about. Don't worry about me, Honey. I'm okay.'

"Sometimes, when boys like these with their head wounds, dictate letters like that I could almost bawl. They are so sweet and so fine to their girls."

Miss De Long is now starting her eighteenth month overseas. She has served the Red Cross in Australia, Milne Bay, Biak, Tacloban in Leyte and now, Manila.

"My work gives me a lot of pleasure," Miss De Long said. "For those letters the wounded boys of ours dictate to their girls back home—they are just beautiful."

« 52 »

A Place to Feel at Home

THE MANILA CLUB is a very nice private club, as good as they come. It has a friendly, homey, delightful atmosphere.

It is GI Joe's own exclusive club in Manila. For it is restricted to enlisted men only. It is the GI's meeting place in Manila, a club where he can feel at home, which makes his three days pass in from the front provide him a better and finer time. So he will never be lonesome and blue in a large, strange city.

It is a very swell club and it was planned, conceived and created by the American Red Cross.

Edwin L. Abbott, 723 Westnedge avenue south, Kalamazoo, the Manila area recreation supervisor for the Red Cross, supervised the founding of the Manila Club.

Ed Abbott is a fine fellow. One of those Red Cross workers who has been up in The Line with the GI's. He knows their requirements when they come in from the front on leave. A place to go. A place to have fun. A place to feel at home at. That's the Manila Club.

And the club is popular with the GI's. Abbott told me that 50,000 GI's visit it every Sunday. On any week day, 30,000 GI's use the club. Over a million GI's are served every month at their club. That's the best yardstick of which I know about how the GI's like it.

The club has three floors, a fourth is being completed, and the Red Cross is considering putting in a roof garden.

Miss Ruth Ann Ryder, of 428 Evergreen avenue, East Lansing, is one of six Red Cross workers who built the club.

"We serve the GI cold drinks and sandwiches and coffee," Miss Ryder said. "But most of all we provide him with a place to sit down in Manila and that's what he wanted most."

Miss Ryder has been overseas 19 months, a veteran Red Cross worker in Australia, New Guinea and the Philippines.

"It took us a month to get the club in shape," she said. "We started working on it March 12, and the club opened April 17. Mrs. MacArthur came to our opening night.

"It was a building that had been stripped of everything when we took it over. Part of the building was uncompleted. There wasn't a chair or a table in the place.

"So all the fixtures and all the furniture and all the furnishings we scrounged from the military forces. They were eager for GI Joe to have this club anyway, and they really co-operated with us.

"When we first started working in the building, I went down to the 37th Engineers. I needed a company of men to work on the place. Why, the engineers were so surprised to see an American woman in the combat zone that they said 'yes' without knowing how much work they were letting themselves in for.

"But they did work hard. I got a kick out of the fact that some of those boys who were helping us had set up American guns on the same scene, guns that fired across the river at the Japs."

Miss Ryder, whose father, E. H. Ryder, was for 35 years a professor at Michigan State College, was also the promoter of the Michigan State College Manila Reunion on June 10.

Mrs. Josephine Weaver Wright, of Grandville, Mich., has an interesting job with the Red Cross. For 21 months overseas she has been an assistant field director in camp service, in Australia and Moresby and Oro Bay in New Guinea. Her specialty is personal problems.

Through Red Cross channels, Mrs. Wright is able to get the information the GI wants and back home the Military Relief and the Red Cross help to iron these problems out.

This service gives the GI a sense of security.

« 53 »

Jungle Juice for GI's

THE PATROLS ALWAYS came back to the outer perimeter defenses of the 13th Air Force, after 15 days in the Jap lines, tired, dirty and thirsty.

As they came in, their helmets muddy, their green fatigues caked with dirt and mud, their rifles hanging nonchalantly from their shoulders, the riflemen always called out to the Red Cross girls waiting for them, "How about some Red Cross Jungle Juice!"

Miss Gertrude Montgomery, of Tecumseh, Mich., who formerly worked for the City of Detroit's recreation department, told me that "jungle juice" was a drink made of fruit syrup and water—and served iced cold.

You have to be in the Orient in wartime to appreciate that phrase "ice cold." Any cold drink in the Philippines is like a pot of gold at the end of a rainbow.

"We would get in a recon car, fill it full of sandwiches and jungle juice," Mis Montgomery said, "when the patrols from the 31st Division were coming in.

"We met the patrols at the outer perimeter. Oh, our boys looked so tired in their full packs. But they always grinned and started to shout for cold drinks when they saw us.

"At first we had cute, dainty little cups to serve the drinks. But the boys just laughed. They brought out those big Army canteen cups and said, 'Fill it up, will you, Beautiful'!

"They were all thirsty for a cold drink. Every one of those boys would stand there, smacking his lips—and drinking about two quarts of our jungle juice.

"It was great fun to serve them. The cold drinks—after all

the awful water they had drunk out on patrols, sometimes anything—refreshed them and made them grin and start wise cracking."

Experience taught the Red Cross girls that the Yank soldier returning from the front is a real hungry and thirsty guy. If they were going to serve 500 soldiers with cold drinks and refreshments, Miss Montgomery said "we always took enough for a thousand, just in case."

"At the 13th Air Force," she continued, "we would go out to the ack-ack gun emplacements in the daytime. The gunners were on duty. We brought them cold drinks and refreshments. Games and comfort articles.

"They were so grateful for everything. But we had to be out of there before dark, before the guns started shooting at any Jap sneak raiders.

"The eternal vigilance these ack-ack boys had to maintain kept them tense. We provided them with a few brief moments of relaxation, I hope."

Miss Montgomery has been 13 months overseas for the Red Cross. She has been in New Guinea, Morotai, the Admiralties, and Manila, now in the personnel department of the Red Cross.

Her specialty is providing recreation for the enlisted men at craft shops and canteens.

"The GI's even helped make our doughnut machines work when they were out of order," she said. "They always helped us. In New Guinea they helped us build their club. They liked that. They are very self-reliant, self-sufficient fellows anyway, and they got a kick out of helping themselves.

"We had quiz shows and movies at our club in New Guinea. And we were right on Milne Bay, where the ocean was so blue and so beautiful.

"It was a wonderful setting for a Red Cross club for enlisted men. But it could never be too good, for these GI's are friendly, nice guys who deserve the best—anywhere."

« 54 »

A Narrow Escape

STORIES ABOUT the Villa Verde are endless.

One night Pfc. Nicholas Laping, 4043 Harding avenue, Detroit, was driving an ambulance without lights and full of wounded Yanks.

Suddenly, the ambulance stalled. Laping could not see even the front fenders. He got out. The wheels were hanging over a cliff!

"We removed our patients," he said, "and carried them down to the portable hospital. There was nothing else to do."

Our Yank patrols always had enough excitement, as they flitted about the enemy lines, to last any ordinary fellow for life.

Sergt. Joseph A. Skiba, 2221 Schoenherr road, Utica, led a patrol of four Yanks and eight Filipino guerillas deep into Jap territory.

The patrol paused for a breather after a long climb. They scouted a Jap patrol to their west, another enemy patrol to the south, and a full Jap platoon moving from the north.

Vastly outnumbered, it had been spotted by the Japs.

The enemy came up slowly on three sides. There was only one escape left, a long, dangerous climb.

Their mission had been to collect information on enemy movements, and return to their lines without provoking a fight.

Skiba broke his patrol into two groups. For hours they climbed. Reaching the top, still undetected by the Japs, they bivouacked. In the morning they looked into the draw. Japs were searching the brush for the patrol!

You might think that being a cook in the Army is a safe job. But the cooks go up forward.

Sergt. Roy B. Webster, of S. Rockwood, Mich., is in charge of the mess detail for the medics of "Baker" Company, 107th Medical Battalion. A Jap infiltration party got within 30 feet of his kitchen, and Jap machine guns several times filled the kitchen tent with holes.

"A Jap sneaked in one night," Sergt. Webster said. "He had hand grenades and satchels of TNT.

"A good thing our guard killed him. He might have blown up the kitchen.

"We always got breakfast on time, for a Jap machine gun used to open up promptly at 6:30 every morning on our camp, just like an alarm clock."

A round-up of the news about some of our Michigan boys.

Pfc. Craig L. Rayl, 159 Richter, River Rouge, has been awarded the Combat Infantry Badge for "exemplary conduct under fire."

George J. Lehman, 5756 Maxwell, Detroit, has been promoted from corporal to staff sergeant, and William E. McVety, of Falmouth, Mich., from private class to corporal.

The Commonwealth Government of the Philippines has awarded the Philippine Liberation medal to Staff Sergt. Joseph L. Horn, 5356 Harding, Detroit, and Pfc. Mario L. Montagna, 8983 May, Detroit.

Some of the real veterans of World War II, now starting their fourth year overseas, include:

Pfc Ralph M. Rose, 3085 Eastern, Detroit.

Staff Sergt. Frank Szacum, a graduate of Hamtramck High School.

Pfc. John H. Snyder, 14252 Sorrento, Detroit, a military policeman.

A number of Detroiters, after basic training in the States, received their battle experience on the Villa Verde. They are real veterans now.

Among these new Detroiters are:

Pvt. Edward J. Morris, 3057 St. Clair; Pvt. Eugene Widelski, a rifleman, 5815 Gilbert; Pvt. Stanislaw Lenski, 6109 Cecil, a rifleman; Pvt. Lloyd W. Lavictoire, 3847 Huron, infantryman; Pvt. Jerome J. Thomas, 2670 Lycaste.

Pvt. Paul F. Ebeling, 13989 Plainview; Pvt. Robert D. Joshua, 2747 Franklin; Pvt. Thomas Fortin, 1292 East Grand boulevard; Pvt. Paul A. Pallagi, whose brother Joe is in the Marines; Pvt. Walter M. Dombrowski, 3970 Lawndale; Pvt. Jospeh J. Radtke, 2275 Warren east.

Pvt. Edward J. Sluck, 4460 Dubois; Pvt. Casimir A. Kwilias, 4203 Martin, and Pvt. Anthony J. Brutz, 23655 Koths avenue, Inkster, Mich.

« 55 »

Ambulance With Wings

THE WOUNDED VETERANS of the 32nd were flown here by L-5's, those capable little ships bought in war bonds by the school children of Detroit, from the Villa Verde front.

I was very glad of that after I made a three-hour jeep ride from the Villa Verde to this great, modern hospital. Believe me, no seriously wounded Yank could have stood that ride by ambulance. The roads were rough, primitive, rocky. It jarred your body and put an ache in your stomach to make that ride in good health.

But our wounded came in by airship, each wounded Red Arrow veteran with a compartment of his own, a 13 to 15-minute plane ride. That was a very good deal.

So I talked to four Michigan nurses at work, all officers of the Army Nurses Corps, all of whom have been overseas for 16 and 17 months.

They had a hearty admiration for the fighting men of the 32nd.

"It is amazing," said Lieut. Madeline L. Dickerson, 25046 Waltham avenue, Detroit, whose folks now live in Petoskey, "it is amazing how much those boys love their Red Arrow Division. They are proud of it."

"To our patients," remarked Lieut. Mary E. Bassett, 20855 Fourteen Mile road, Birmingham, Mich., who used to be a nurse at Henry Ford Hospital, "the 32nd is the only division in the world. They told me how much fighting it has done. It really is a great division."

I talked to doctors, to orderlies, to enlisted men working as medical aids in the wards. The same story. These mountain men of the 32nd believe their division is not only the best in the American Forces, but also invincible. To them the division means everything. There is something magnificent in the pride which our boys take in being with the 32nd.

I heard a veteran sergeant talking to a green replacement who had just moved up to the front in a troop carrier.

"You're with the 32nd now, Bub," said the giant sergeant. "Don't worry about nothin', nothin' at all. We'll take care of you!"

When you hear things like that it makes your heart sing. These boys of ours are so far from home, 10,000 long, dreary miles; they have been fighting for 38 months in seven rough campaigns. They have smashed the Jap everywhere they have met him. And in the division there is a comradely spirit that makes the college fraternities seem like tiddly-wink clubs.

Our nurses have worked hard for the wounded; long hours, 12 and 15 hours a day, and under pressure by the enemy, too. For the Japs are always sneaking in at night and trying to blow up the wounded and kill the nurses and doctors.

For the Jap ignores all the rules of civilized war.

I stood in the cool corridor of the field hospital, which currently had 600 patients from four fighting divisions, talking with Lieuts. Dickerson and Bassett; Lieut. Elaine Naomi Ntceros, 451 Norwood southeast, Grand Rapids, and Lieut. Doris A. Adams, of Homer, Mich., who likewise took her nurse's training at Henry Ford Hospital in Detroit.

"Twice a night," said Lieut. Adams, "throughout the first month here, we could hear the Japs, down by the road, back in the hills. They were always sneaking out on the roads near us. We had ground alerts. We slept in the hospital. Several nights we couldn't sleep. The Japs were that close. But our boys always got them, sometime or other."

"The troops killed some Japs a half a mile away last night," reported Lieut. Elaine Ntceros.

"We don't pay much attention to them when they are two or three miles away," observed Lieut. Bassett.

"Gee whiz," said Lieut. Dickerson, "some of us were coming in from Manila. We crossed a bridge about eight miles down the road. An MP with a tommy-gun stopped our jeep and said, 'Did you see anything?' We hadn't seen a thing. He said, 'You're lucky, girls, there are 30 Japs over there in a field. You came right by them.' Gosh, can you imagine that!"

"Well, it was exciting," said Lieut. Adams.

"We have had quite a few Detroit patients," said Lieut. Bassett. "I certainly was pleased one day. A combat engineer was in my ward with a shell wound. He said he used to watch me get on a bus! He was such a nice boy."

"The boys from the Red Arrow are all nice," said Lieut. Adams.

« 56 »

Cause for Hatred

THE MEN OF THE 32ND—from platoon scout to rifleman, from mortar sections to artillery batteries, from the demolition assault troopers to the bazooka men—hate the Japs with a bitter hatred.

Perhaps this story itself, from the lips of Michigan men, will explain. It is merely one of many reasons.

At San Fabian after the landings by Gen. MacArthur's Forces in Lingayen Gulf, the 43rd Field Hospital was setting up for wounded due from the battlefield.

A hospital like this one is not a fighting unit. When the Japs hit, there were less than a dozen guards. And for five and one-half hours the fight went on.

Whereupon, the men of the 32nd hit them on one flank.

Troops came rushing up from somewhere and hit them on the other flank. They killed many Japs, and what were left alive were driven back, away from the hospital.

"I jumped into a ditch when the Jap machine guns opened up," related Sergt. Hans H. Gadebusch, of 28803 Nine Mile road, Farmington, Mich. "That was the only thing I could do. In the first blast they wounded and killed 10 of our men. I am a laboratory technician, not a fighting man. But all of us know how to keep our heads down."

Pfc. Don Amato, 3020 Tyler, Detroit, a medical technician, found himself "right in the midst of the fighting."

"I got out of the ditch to help carry some of the wounded back where we could treat them," Amato said. "The Japs banged away at us even then. The next day you should have seen my tent. It looked like a Swiss cheese."

"We got into that mess," said Corp. Joseph L. Monroe, 1465 Lakepointe road, Grosse Pointe, Mich., "because it was about D plus 10 (eleventh day after the landing), and we had to get set up close."

Staff Sergt. Frank Butykos, of 436 South West End, Detroit, the mess sergeant, said he "lay there watching the scrap."

"The next morning we had chow as usual," Sergt. Butykos said. "Even if the Japs did shoot up our kitchen, Jap bullets can't interfere with chow. When the Army has to eat, it has to eat.

"In our setup here, we now feed 750 three meals a day. In Hollandia, we fed 1,300 daily."

"It takes a lot of cooking over our field ranges," said Sergt. Ernest W. Hallenbeck, of 604 Finley avenue, Big Rapids, Mich., the hospital's cook.

I couldn't resist asking how the hospital mess was.

"It's very good for the combat zone," said Corp. Monroe.

"Well, we had fried chicken—chicken right from the states, so much more tender than these Luzon chicks—three times last month," said Sergt. Hallenbeck. "Quite often we have steaks, good American steaks."

"But most important of all in this climate," said Sergt. Butykos, "we have ice and we have ice water and iced lemonade all the time."

He wasn't just talking. I promptly drank a full canteen cup of ice-cold lemonade. It's funny how values change over here. That was a very simple, unimportant drink back home. Probably cost you 10 cents at a drug counter. But it seemed to make life more like living, that canteen cup full of ice-cold lemonade.

Of course it was very hot that day.

« 57 »

Smiling Through Cakes of Mud

THE TRUCK TROOP CARRIERS were coming down the hairpin turns of the Villa Verde Trail where the Red Arrow Division has been fighting for 125 days in a smashing campaign that wiped out almost 9,000 Japs.

The infantrymen were standing up, laughing and shouting. The GI is a mercurial fellow. He can adapt himself to any hazards. He takes the hell of the front lines as so much routine.

The herringbone-twill combat uniforms of our boys were caked with mud. So were their helmets. So were their combat boots. So were their faces. Only their rifles, their own insurance policies against death in combat, were clean and shining.

They were singing songs, and they were very gay. They sang raucous GI songs and the love songs of Tin Pan Alley.

They waved captured Jap sabers and captured Jap rifles. Some of them perched Jap helmets on their heads. They tied Jap battle flags to the trucks.

You can tell a winning division on the march!

These boys had the smile of victory on their faces. They were tired, yes. They had fought all day; stayed awake most of the night in foxholes, alerted for Jap infiltration parties. They stood in foxholes with water up to their knees.

They had experienced everything in mountain war—a war by squads, fought at 15 feet, at hand to hand, and they had not only defeated but annihilated the Japs. They cut up the Jap companies in a good drubbing.

Our boys knew what they had done. Some of them were veterans of many campaigns. Some of them were new. The Villa Verde was their first campaign. They had been worried and fretful as they first went into action. Now they were veterans, too.

It was good to see them laugh again. It was good to hear them sing. It was nice to know that Maj.-Gen. W. H. Gill, their commander, had arranged a delightful rest camp for those men not at the front, with the beach of the Pacific a base ball's toss from camp. Sunlight. Rest. Swimming. Fun. That's what Gill said his men needed.

I had been with Gill at the front. I had had long chats with him at night in his mountain camp. I knew his concern for these soldiers. He knew they had been in the line for weeks. He knew it took something out of their stamina.

Yet the days of the campaign were full of excitement. Medals were awarded, many of them for the Villa Verde fight, still others for the Leyte campaign that preceded it.

One Detroit soldier was happy as he came down the Villa Verde. The Silver Star is hard to win because it is only won by gallantry in action. Sergt. Robert F. Jeffrey, of 1319 Somerset avenue, Grosse Pointe Park, won it in Leyte; got it on the Villa Verde.

This Detroiter destroyed two Jap tanks that had pierced the Yank perimeter, disregarding his personal safety. Pfc. Jeffrey saw the Jap tanks rumbling along a road leading to a vital Yank supply dump. He grabbed a bazooka, crept up toward the tanks. The Japs spotted him. They fear and hate bazooka men. They opened fire with their tank cannons and tank machine guns.

Jeffrey escaped the fire. He fired his bazooka. His first shot was a direct hit on the lead Jap tank, killing the crew and destroying the tank.

Jeffrey was cool. The Jap machine guns were trying to find him. But he blasted away, got the second tank.

Two other Michigan boys were awarded the Silver Star,

Second Lieut. Elmer S. Geik, of 352 Ohio street, Benton Harbor, and Pfc. Albert Dutch, of Holland.

Lieut. Geik led a squad of litter bearers through Jap artillery and machine fire to the front lines near Mt. Imugan on the flank of the Villa Verde. He evacuated the last of a group of wounded along the sky line of a bald ridge, while Nip machine gunners put a concentration of fire on his party.

Finding a small gully, Geik took his litter bearers and the wounded into it, safe from enemy bullets. There they administered blood plasma to the wounded.

Dutch, armed with a Browning automatic rifle, spearheaded an attack on an enemy hill position off the Villa Verde. Japs hidden in the kunai grass threw two hand grenades at him but he escaped injury.

A Jap then lobbed four blocks of TNT tied to a hand grenade at Dutch. The lad from Holland was blown 12 feet in the air. He was stunned for a moment, but escaped with a slight concussion.

Dutch picked himself up, shook himself, and pushed forward. With his Browning, he helped capture three Jap light and heavy machine guns.

The next morning he was out with an assault platoon. He knocked out two Jap machine guns in pill boxes. Dutch has 24 Japs to his score.

A Bronze Star Medal for meritorious performance in action was awarded to Pfc. John H. Snyder, Jr., 14252 Sorrento street, Detroit, for controlling traffic over the 25 miles of the Villa Verde Trail.

« 58 »

To Marcos, the Igorot

THE RAINY SEASON is really here now.

The rain was coming down in a torrential flow. It was a cold rain. Like almost everything in the climate of the Philippines, it made everyone uncomfortable.

Officers of the cavalry recon troop put down the canvas sides of their squad tent, lit a Coleman camping lamp, and gaily opened a can of shrimp. We dipped it in some tomato soup.

"Pretty good," said Lieut. Louis J. Wortham, of Center, Tex., the recon commander.

Earlier in the afternoon I had been chinning with some Detroit soldiers.

Pfc. Delbert F. Graves, 5447 Fourth, Detroit, had shot and killed a Jap officer on Christmas morning, and sent the captured saber back home to his wife.

He was a rifleman with I Company, 127th Infantry, during the Villa Verde push. Graves recalled they were "pushing up a hill."

Corp. Bruce D. Allow, 81 Mapleton road, Grosse Pointe Farms, was listening. He was a cannoneer with the 121st Field Artillery's batteries of 155's for a long time.

"I had all my excitement at Biak," he said. "We were right up at the front, in holes. A mortar hit on the edge of my hole —but missed. A knee mortar hit between a guy's legs in the next foxhole and didn't go off. That's the way things go."

At division headquarters, I stopped to talk to Sergt. Clarence A. Brosteau, 259 Reginald south, Dearborn.

"That first night at Saidor," he said, "I was lying in my bunk when a Jap plane came over. I said to myself, 'Here it is!' I hugged the ground. I heard one bomb go off nearby. I guess that was my initiation."

Wortham had just given me a silver ring with the insignia of the Red Arows.

"Hey, Nel," he said, "tell him about our boy Marcos."

Lieut Ivan C. Nelson, of Merrill, Wis., got a shrimp out of the can with deft fingers.

"Marcos is the best damned fightin' man, pound for pound, in the world," Nelson said.

"Get him, Nel," said Wortham.

Nelson buried himself in a poncho and started out in the rain.

"Marcos is one of our Igorot scouts, our chief scout," said Wortham. "He is the best I ever saw. Tireless. Uncanny. Let me tell you about him."

Nelson came back with Marcos. The Igorot was dressed like an Army Joe. He grinned often, his teeth flashing.

He was five feet and weighed 120. But he was built like a big man in miniature. As he shook hands, his grip had steel springs in it.

"I like American Army," he said. "Marcos is proud to be a scout."

They gave him a bottle of beer. Nelson stared at him.

"The other day on Yamashita Ridge, he showed a twelfth sense," Nelson said. "Two scouts went by. Said something was wrong. Marcos looked at the trail. He said, 'Five Japs. Ten minutes. Three yards away.' Sure enough. We went down in the trail and got them!" Marcos grinned some more.

"Another day," said Wortham, "old Marcos—he is 28 and looks older, doesn't he?—was out ahead of a patrol, his carbine slung on his shoulder, chasing retreating Japs, right on their grenades."

Marcos laughed. "Yank grenades good," he said, "very good."

"He's a sharp one," Nel said. "We get out in the Jap hills. Lot of tension. Always danger of being cut off. We heard wood chopping 30 yards away near a creek bed. Marcos said, 'Two men. Cutting wood. Civilians. Not Japs. Jap makes different chopping sound.'"

Marcos just grinned.

"When we fight Japs again, Boss?" he asked Wortham.

"Soon, you bloodthirsty little guy," Wortham replied. "Now off with you. Get back to your family. Bring your two kids over tomorrow."

Marcos took off in the rain.

"Great little guy," concluded Wortham. "They don't come any better. His wife does the laundry for the troop. We want her to make some money. She jawed away at Marcos because she had no flat iron."

"And what do you think that little guy did?"

"Well, long before we took Imugan, he just went out in the bush, crawled into Imugan, right into the Jap lines, went to his old home, dug up a flat iron—and brought it in!"

Nel opened some more beer.

"To Marcos the Igorot!" said Wortham.

Well, the recon troop is an amazing bunch of men.

« 59 »

78 Heroes Receive Medals

THE NAVY FLYING patrol boat flew crew at tree-top level. Whereupon, the Red Arrow band played the Star Spangled Banner.

The 78 heroes of the 32nd Division stood at attention in two long rows of bronzed fighting men, the veterans of the Villa Verde Trail.

They stood as men apart in the ceremony dedicated to their gallantry in action against the Japs. They stood before Maj.-Gen. W. H. Gill, commander of this great division.

Behind them stood the five companies of the 3rd Battalion, 128th Regiment, commanded by Lieut.-Col. Douglas E. Des Rosier, of 1675 Webb, Detroit. The battalion was the guard of honor, chosen for its bitter fighting in the Villa Verde campaign.

Lieut.-Col. Edward W. Hoffman, of San Antonio, Tex., the division's adjutant-general, stood before the microphone of the public address system, reading off the citations.

On the right side of the parade ground, other Red Arrow veterans stood as interested spectators.

It took a long time to read all those 78 names, but no one seemed to mind.

Behind Gill stood his staff at attention. Col. E. A. Barlow, chief of staff, from Salt Lake City; Lieut.-Col. George A. Bond, Jr., San Angelo, Tex.; Maj. E. G. Boyer, of Lansing, Mich., and Chief Warrant Officer Morris Samsky, 2005 Philadelphia west, Detroit.

GI's began taking snapshots as Gill walked briskly to the head of the line where the 78 veterans stood. For all of these men were going back home on rotation. Some of their GI pals wanted a last snapshot of them as they were decorated.

An aid handed Gill a Distinguished Service Cross, and the division commander pinned it on the left breast of Sergt. Richard J. Pieh, of Deerfield, Mich., who won the award for "extraordinary heroism connected with military action against the enemy."

"Good job, sergeant," the General said, smiling.

The Michigan sergeant stood at attention, his face immobile, but his eyes danced beneath his helmet.

Gill turned to decorate seven Silver Star winners for gallantry in action. Three of them were from Michigan, including:

Corp. Carl Leichwise, 146 Ferris, Highland Park.

Pfc. Casimir Czyzewski, 313 Richards, Kalamazoo.

Pfc. Edward E. Regan, 305 Milwaukee north, Jackson.

Sixteen other Michigan soldiers were awarded the Bronze Star for meritorious achievement in combat against the enemy. They were:

Lieut. Jack A. Clark, 1259 Cavalry, Detroit; Sergt. Edward T. Hart, 385 Eason, Highland Park; Sergt. Earl H. Pett, 2483 Van Dyke, Detroit; Sergt. Robert M. Lovell, of Leonard.

Sergt. Joseph A. Skiba, Utica; Sergt. George J. Tulauskas, 793 Channing, Ferndale; Sergt. Clarence H. Wade, 701 Court, Sault Ste. Marie; Sergt. Walter F. Munger, 427 Seventh west, Flint.

Sergt. John Thomas, 9739 Mt. Elliott, Detroit; Sergt. Dominic Vallone, 3510 Sheridan, Detroit; Corp. Raymond R. Grit, 1143 Cass, Grand Rapids; Corp. Chester Czarmonski, 6462 Craig, Detroit.

Corp. Harry L. Fowler, 3801 Humboldt, Detroit; Corp. Emil S. Magier, 5633 Martin, Detroit; Corp. Henry T. Stephenson, 332 Burke, River Rouge; Pfc. John L. McAlpine, Ypsilanti.

The General returned to the high ground, and the 78 marched proudly down the field, stood at attention on his left. With the division band playing, the five companies of Col. Des Rosier's battalion of honor marched past the 78 heroes, past Gill, dipping their blue guidons.

"They march well. Fine group of fighting men, fine!" Gill remarked.

The battalion took its place at the General's right. Behind them, watching every marching man with interest, stood Col.

Merle H. Howe, of Grand Rapids, commander of the 128th Regiment.

It was the kind of a ceremony that the Red Arrow Division will long remember. There are things that fighting men treasure for all time. And talk about years later when they are veterans back home in their easy chairs.

This was something to remember. The ceremony made your heart sing. For these veterans looked so grand. They had been fighting for 125 days on the Villa Verde. They won their campaign against all odds of terrain, climate and Jap defensive tactics. Now they paid honor to their 78 heroes.

« 60 »

With a Catch in His Voice

A TWO-STAR GENERAL is too busy with the military details of an operation like the Villa Verde Trail campaign to get an opportunity to speak to all of his fighting men.

There are times when he would like to talk to each of his men, especially when they have a tough fight like that on the Villa Verde, especially when 78 current heroes are going home on rotation.

So at the grand ceremony for the decorating of the 78, including 20 veterans from Michigan, Maj.-Gen. W. H. Gill, commander of the Red Arrow Division, stepped briskly to the microphone to address these soldiers, so once and for all they could carry with them the memory of what their commanding officer thought of them.

Gen. Gill spoke straightforward from the heart, not in the words of an orator but the words of a fighting general.

Several times there was a catch of emotion in his voice. You knew, by his voice, his manner, by his words, that these men he loved like a father.

He stamped on his half-smoked cigaret and he took off his helmet as he began to speak.

I knew something about how Gen. Gill felt about his men. At night on the Villa Verde I had sat with him in his tent while he worried about his men's health, about the tough, hard life they led in their foxholes.

Now he was before the microphone, with the 78 heroes at his left, the battalion guard of honor at his right, and thousands of rugged soldiers listening.

"Men," Gen. Gill said, "go ahead if you wish to smoke. Sit down if you care to. I simply want to say" . . . and there was a catch in his voice . . . "to these men of ours who are going home, goodby and happy landings. I am going to miss you in the days to come.

"I thank each of the officers and the men for the grand job they have done, a job that has made the 32nd the best division in the Southwest Pacific.

"You have done your job well. Many of you have fought through the Papuan campaign. All of you through the Australian campaign."

There was a swell of laughter which swept across the parade ground at this reference to "the Australian campaign," where many Yanks married Australian girls.

"Still it paid big dividends—our re-equipping and re-organizing in Australia—dividends at Saidor, Aitape, Drinimure River, Leyte and on Luzon.

"You men of this division have made a record you can well be proud of. All of those places have memories for you and for me.

"Those memories will be valuable to you in the years to come. When you are old and gray these memories will live with you to inspire you.

"Your co-operation, your hard work, your magnificent performance — for these things, please accept my heartfelt thanks."

Gen. Gill paused for a moment. His sharp eyes swept through the ranks of the 78, through the battalion guard of honor, out across the parade field to the ranks of many men.

"Remember," he resumed, "wherever your divided paths may lead, you are always Red Arrow men. You have an enviable record. Don't let anyone argue with you about what your division has accomplished. If they insist, close it up!"

A wave of laughter swept over the field. This was a fighting man's language to fighting men and they liked it and understood it.

"Wherever the Red Arrow flag flies—you are always welcome.

"To you men going home, good luck!

"Remember, God has been good to most of you. May he continue to walk by you. Adios!"

« 61 »

Michigan Heroes Rate High

OUR MICHIGAN BOYS looked very good as they stood before their division commander. Four days out of combat, Maj. Gen. W. H. Gill, commander of the Red Arrow, was decorating 78 heroes with medals.

Twenty Michigan boys were there, with the eyes of the division upon them, the band playing "Roses and Orchids," and the battalion guard of honor dipping its blue guidons.

First to be decorated was Sergt. Richard J. Pieh, of Deerfield, Mich., who was awarded the Distinguished Service Cross for "extraordinary heroism in action against the enemy."

Sergt. Pieh's company attacked and was stopped short by Japs in more than 50 fortified positions. Pieh grabbed a machine gun and advanced boldly on the Japs. His entire company was inspired, and they smashed the Japs in front of them, consolidating their lines.

The Silver Star for gallantry was awarded to Sergt. Carl Leichwise, 146 Ferris, Highland Park; Pfc. Edward E. Reagan, Jackson, and Pfc. Casimir Czyzewski, of Kalamazoo.

Sergt. Leichwise, a medical aid man, went from foxhole to foxhole, under intense artillery, automatic weapons and sniper fire, directing the evacuation of the wounded.

Pfc. Reagan found booby traps, dug out mines and helped clear the Ormoc highway for the tanks. During this, Jap snipers peppered away at him.

Pfc. Czyzewski charged an enemy dugout with fixed bayonet. Several enemy positions opened up on him but he killed all four Japs in the dugout.

Bronze Stars for meritorious achievement were awarded:

Sergt. Emil S. Magier, 5633 Martin, Detroit: His half-track was stopped by a Jap road block. He wiped out a light machine gun nest.

Sergt. Henry T. Stephenson, 130 Maple, River Rouge: He made night ambulance runs on the Villa Verde Trail with the wounded, in a complete blackout.

Corp. Chester Czarnomski, 6462 Craig, Detroit: One of three ambulance drivers ambushed. The lead vehicle was sprayed by bullets at 50 feet. Undiscouraged by this, he continued to evacuate the wounded under fire.

Sergt. Dominic Vallone, 3510 Sheridan, Detroit, an ambulance driver: He made repeated night runs from the farthest forward aid station down. Because of a road slide, he had to carry his patients part of the way under fire.

Sergt. John Thomas, 9739 Mt. Elliott, Detroit: He had to go up to the front and repair vehicles under enemy fire.

Sergt. George J. Tulauskas, 793 Channing, Ferndale: He administered first aid and evacuated wounded under fire.

Sergt. Earl H. Pett, 2483 Van Dyke, Detroit: On two occasions he handled the ammunition supply for a task force with little assistance from outside his section.

Sergt. Edward T. Hart, 385 Eason, Highland Park: For military operations from New Guinea to the Philippines, he supervised and insured the efficient operation of the inspector-general's section as chief clerk.

First Lieut. Jack A. Clark, 1259 Cavalry, Detroit: He organized the first code school ever to be started while a division was in combat.

Corp. Harry I. Fowler, 6006 Twelfth, Detroit: As a messenger, he was with forward echelons at Buna, Aitape, Leyte and Luzon operations.

Pfc. John L. McAlpine, Ypsilanti: On a dark night, McAlpine was evacuating patients in his ambulance which ran off the road, stopped, was suspended on the front axle, its wheels overhanging a cliff. He carried patients on litters to the portable hospital.

Sergt. Robert M. Lovell, Leonard, Mich.: As headquarters communications sergeant, he kept communications going through adverse conditions.

Sergt. Walter F. Munger, Flint: He remained at his post, despite enemy shelling, directing the movement of vehicles.

Sergt. Joseph A. Skiba, Utica: He made 50 patrol missions, displaying "meritorious and outstanding performance of duty."

Sergt. Clarence H. Wade, Sault Ste. Marie: The division's crack band was organized under his leadership.

Corp. Jacob B. Caldwell, 18280 Prairie, Detroit: Despite air attacks, he was responsible for the maintenance of vehicles for the division's forward command post.

« 62 »

Jap Atrocities Invade a Dream

THIS IS A STORY about a sergeant who screamed in his sleep one morning—and why.

You wouldn't expect Staff Sergt. William S. Seifert, of York, Pa., to be so unnerved that he would ever scream in his sleep.

As chief of the litter section for Company A of the 107th Medical Battalion, Seifert spent 140 days in the combat zone on the Villa Verde Trail and in the drive up highway No. 5 into the Cagayan Valley.

"What I saw and heard one night," he said, "was so terrible I shall never forget it. As long as I live I shall hate the Japs . . . forever!"

It happened on the Villa Verde. Seifert was with the battalion command post of a fighting regiment when it set up its perimeter defense against Jap night banzai attacks.

The battalion's telephone suddenly failed. Five linemen of the Signal Corps went out to find the break. They found it. Several of them bent over to see what happened. The Japs had cut the line!

The realization came just as a Jap light machine gun roared. The Japs ambushed the linemen. Three were killed. One crawled away to safety. One went down, wounded.

Seven Japs pounced on the wounded GI. They carried him into a hole. All this happened only 50 feet away from the Yank perimeter defense.

Then came the screams of Jap atrocity—the screams of an American victim.

"I could hear the hissing yelling of the Japs," said Seifert.

"And then came terrible screams—screams I shall never forget—from our wounded rifleman.

"He was yelling for help. It was the most helpless feeling I ever had. I knew he was being tortured. In a few seconds, 30 of our riflemen formed a volunteer patrol. They went out after our man.

"The Japs opened up with their machine guns. Our boys closed in—mad, angry. They cut those Nips to ribbons. The Japs had the best of it, machine guns against rifles and hand grenades, but our boys were just mad—plenty mad."

Seifert and Corp. Harold A. Beauregard, 3471 Bishop avenue, Detroit, litter bearers, went along with the patrol. They ducked the Jap bullets. They had no weapons, of course, but they carried a litter. They wanted to save that tortured Yank if they could.

They carried him out. All the medical facilities of that sector of the front were mobilized in 30 seconds.

He had 30 bayonet wounds in his chest and stomach and neck. Before he drifted into unconsciousness, he whispered: "Tied my hands; feet. Eased bayonets into me. Slowly. An inch at a time. They were—devils."

That story went along through the GI grapevine. Every soldier in the battalion knew it. They had heard the screams. Some saw the tortured Yank brought in.

Our boys of the 32nd are tough and rough. They were waiting in their foxholes. They knew a certain order would come.

Seifert knew it would come, too. He fell asleep in his foxhole. He woke up screaming, with Beauregard shaking him.

"My God," he said, "in my sleep I could see those Japs slowly stabbing that American boy to death with bayonets. That nightmare was so vivid, so clear, I just screamed."

The battalion attacked at dawn—mad, angry, furious. The battalion cut the Jap defenders to pieces.

Officers did not have to call on the mortars and the artillery that day. With hand grenades, bazookas and flame-throwers, with rifles and TNT demolition charges, these angry Yanks stormed ahead.

It is too bad their dead pal, the young 23-year-old tortured rifleman, never knew. But his epitaph was written that day in the angry courage of his own troops.

And when you hear stories like this, and there are so many, you must know that the American doughboy, the footslogger, is a magnificent soldier!

« 63 »

A Memory of Luzon

THERE WAS A SOLEMN grandeur that rainy, cloudy afternoon about the memorial ceremony dedicated to the memory of the members of the 127th Infantry of the Red Arrow Division who were killed in action on the Villa Verde Trail.

It was a ceremony which seemed at the moment to symbolize the feelings of the entire division, from GI Joe to the commanding general, for its dead.

It made me feel, as I listened and watched, that I would remember it forever. It was that kind of a ceremony—a last farewell by the fighting men who lived to the fighting men who had died in action.

Our heavy bombers were flying low overhead, due to the overcast sky, while the American flag flew at half mast on the flagstaff.

Before the ceremonies began, Col. Frederick R. Stofft, of Tucson, Ariz., the regimental commander, remarked to me in a low voice for such a stalwart fighting officer, "This is the price we pay."

His eyes swept the rows and rows of white crosses, over the

seven acres of American graves. In them there was an ineffable sadness. "Many of my officers and men are out there," he said, "many of them."

Maj.-Gen. W. H. Gill, the commanding general of the Red Arrow, stood at ramrod attention, with his staff, facing a flag-draped coffin. Six picked men, every one of whom had done the impossible at the front on many occasions, stood beside it.

A guard of honor, in battle dress, with their Garands on their shoulders, stood at attention. Back of them stood the escort guard of 50 picked veterans, fighting men chosen from every company of the 127th.

All these veterans had friends and pals with whom they had trained in the States four years ago, when they were greenhorn soldiers erupted out of civilian life; and with whom they had fought for 38 months on the long road back from Buna to the Philippines.

The faces of these veterans were serious. This was no routine Army ceremony. You could see that in their faces.

And they were not alone. Col. Stofft and all the ranking officers stood at the head of his men. And over on the sidelines, crowded together in long lines, standing at attention, were hundreds of the veterans of the 127th.

No one had asked them to come. No one had ordered them to come. They came by jeep. They came by truck. A long, rough, three-hour ride in the rain to the ceremony. They had friends out there lying under those white crosses.

Later, I learned there were some Detroit veterans in the escort guard of honor. After the ceremony was over and the rains of the Philippines came again, I talked to them.

I found Sergt. Robert E. Jeffrey, 1319 Somerset, Grosse Pointe Park; Sergt. Lawrence R. Ortkras, 8847 Pinehurst, Detroit; Sergt. James C. Crucian, 4655 Russell, and Pfc. Stanley J. Bahoski, 6029 Braden.

"One of my pals is out there," Sergt. Jeffrey said. "A great guy. I've been wanting to come here a long time."

The ceremony itself would have given the folks back home, the parents, the wives, the relatives of these dead Yanks, a lift. They would have seen, could they have been here, what Gen. Gill meant when he told me, "There are no unknown soldiers in unknown graves in the 32nd Division."

« 64 »

A Villa Verde Jeep

THIS CONCERNS a real veteran of the war in the Southwest Pacific with the Red Arrow Division, a veteran battered and worn—a jeep.

It is a cavalry jeep which has seen more fighting and been in more combat than I hope I ever know. If it could talk, its story would be a sensation.

GI's from Michigan claim that it has become the best known jeep in the division.

For one day Lieut.-Col. George A. Bond, Jr., of the commanding general's staff, summoned me to division forward, and presented me with the jeep. It was one of those gay conspiracies among Maj.-Gen. W. H. Gill, commander of the division; Col. E. A. Barlow, chief of staff, and Bond.

"The division wants you to have your own jeep while you are with us," Col. Bond said, "and here it is, a trifle battered —but a real war jeep. Take it down to ordnance."

When I got to ordnance, the boys were waiting for me. Sergt. Steve Szeregnyi, of 5970 Vivian avenue, Dearborn, who worked as a machine repairman for the Ford Rouge plant and has for 26 months overseas been a vehicle mechanic, tuned up the motor for me.

Staff Sergt. Loren C. Craig, of Whitewater, Wis., an ordnance welder, gave me a lock and a big chain. Pvt. Wilfird B. Doiron, of Niagara Falls, N. Y., got out his stencils and his spray gun.

When I left the 732nd Ordnance, under the windshield of the jeep was emblazoned its name in giant white letters, "The Detroit News," with a giant red arrow (the division's insignia) pointing to the name.

I drove many miles toward division forward again. A two and one-half ton truck skidded into a halt, a truck driver from Arkansas roared, "Hey, the Tigers are leading the American League."

When you're so far away from home, such things are good to hear.

As I raced to the parking lot in a cloud of dust at division forward, Warrant Officer Gordon C. Snyder, chief clerk of the adjutant-general's office, stopped in his tracks.

"Boy, that's good to see from my home town," he said, for he lives at 15770 Mendota, Detroit. He won the Bronze Star for meritorious achievement in the Leyte campaign. "It reminds me of home," he added, "seeing your jeep. By the way, my wife sends me all your clippings on the Villa Verde Trail."

I went in to thank the general, the chief of staff, and Col. Bond. When I came out Pfc. John J. Pickarek, 18623 Pelkey, Detroit, was snapping a picture of The Detroit News with his camera.

"Funny thing to take a picture of," I said.

"Aw," said Pfc. Pickarek, a big, hardy fellow, "it reminds me of home—Detroit. I almost dropped dead when I saw that crate parked there."

I was going through a Filipino barrio a few days later when a big MP stopped me. I thought I must be in trouble.

"Hey you, from Detroit," said Sergt. Herman H. Toussaint, of Northville, Mich., who has been overseas for 38 months, "what does Michigan look like?"

And that's the way it's been for two weeks. My gosh, I'm glad the General thought it would be fun to get The Detroit News put on the jeep. It has been fun. For I get lonesome, too, but you're never completely lonesome, 10,600 miles away from the City Hall when the boys from Detroit find you.

I was pulling out of the roadway of our camp late one afternoon when a command car jammed on the brakes. Out popped Lieut. Verne G. Jubenville, a former Detroit policeman.

"If this jeep isn't a sight for sore eyes," he said. "I haven't seen anybody or anything from home in so long."

Corp. Jack Glickoff, 3741 Collingwood, Detroit, with the 128th Regimental Headquarters Company, saw The Detroit News jeep parked one day, and looked me up.

We had a swell talk. Glickoff has been overseas 38 months. He has been on patrols beyond the front lines. He has carried the wounded out.

That battered jeep has become about my best friend, I guess. I never thought of writing a story about it until tonight. I came out of supply headquarters of the 107th Medical Battalion with lotion to ease the discomfort of the prickly heat of the Philippines.

And there were the Calhoun brothers posing for their picture alongside the jeep.

They looked a lot alike, both tall and husky and looking like they could handle any situation. A GI from Pennsylvania took snapshots of Sergt. Harold W. Calhoun, who has done a grand job for medical supply for 38 months and banged away with a tommy gun at the Japs before he joined the medics, and Motor Machinist's Mate Douglas T. Calhoun, a member of the crew of a Coast Guard picket boat who has already had a year's service on the Atlantic Ocean.

"We hadn't seen each other in 40 months," Sergt. Cal said with the widest grin I ever saw. "Then he comes into Manila, gets a few leave days and hitch-hikes all these miles out here."

"We just thought for old time's sake we'd send the folks a picture of us—together again—in front of a real Detroit jeep," the Coast Guardsman said.

"And I'm going to start home on rotation in four days—to get married," his brother added.

Sergt. Cal said that when he gets home the wedding bells would ring, if That Certain Party, Miss Marge Brys, of 1797 Brys drive, Grosse Pointe Woods is "still willing."

His brother slapped him on the back. "Don't worry, kid," he said, "I saw her when I was home on leave—you lucky stiff."

I never saw two fellows so happy. They talked and they laughed and they slapped each other on the back. Then they would just stare at each other.

And suddenly I thought that the darned old jeep was really something.

« 65 »

Vivid Memories For Home

THESE ARE DAYS when many veterans of the Red Arrow Division are saying goodbye to the Southwest Pacific. Some of the first veterans of the division are homeward bound.

On the way home—after 38 months in the Southwest Pacific, after Buna, Saidor, Aitape, the Drenimoor River; after Australia, New Guinea, Leyte and Luzon; after the current operation on the Villa Verde. Home means a lot to these veterans. Some have shown me pictures of their children they have never seen face-to-face.

I know a young private first class who every night writes a nursery sketch with a drawing to his small son.

An officer and his wife write long letters about their three children, calling them by their first names—of children still unborn.

For 38 months is a long, long time to be away from home. But our boys are going back with vivid memories, some amusing, some full of pathos and tragedy, and others etched by adventure.

"When we rolled out of the Golden Gate," said Pfc. Walter F. Wiktor, 5499 Proctor, Detroit, "we never knew we'd be gone 38 months. We were too seasick to care. Most of us thought we'd be gone maybe a year. But 38 months—whew!"

The division arrived in Australia at a hectic time when the Japs were expected to invade at any moment. But they never did. The Battle of the Coral Sea stopped them. The division went to New Guinea and won the stirring Battle of Buna.

"I've been collecting currency and coins," said Sergt. Anthony Piskorski, 2311 Danforth, Hamtramck. "Jap invasion stuff, the Mickey Mouse money, bills from New Guinea, Australia and the Philippines."

It's funny what our boys think of as they review the campaigns they have been through.

"I'm never going to forget," said Sergt. Dominic Vallone, 3510 Sheridan, Detroit, "that our division was the first in the American Armed Forces to launch and land an airborne combat team."

"But since then we've been a lot of mountain goats, fighting in the mountains," said Sergt. Edwin L. Kipp, of Grand Blanc.

"The Red Arrow," continued Vallone, "landed an entire regiment near Buna Mission. The planes dumped us out on the strip with our equipment, took off, didn't even cut out their engines. Everything we used, from mosquito bars to ammo and food, was landed by air."

It was very primitive country with "fuzzy-wuzzies" recruited as litter bearers and pack carriers. As Corp. Roger L. Santure, of 302 Fourth east, Monroe, pointed out, the natives never deserted a wounded Yank.

Here is what some of the other veterans had to say:

Corp. Leonard T. Kucinski, 6236 Grandy, Detroit: "Mud, always mud, as thick as glue, was our worst enemy in the jungles. We strung our hospital tents between coconut trees. A stake wouldn't hold in the mud. Surgeons worked at night by flashlight, ankle deep in the mud."

Sergt. Robert H. Miley, Detroit: "I helped carry a wounded general out on a litter. We carried him two miles through the mud. One short litter bearer went clean out of sight—he stepped in a deep hole."

Pfc. Rex W. Castle, who worked once for Kelsey Hayes Wheel Company of Detroit: "We spent 36 hours under bombardment by Jap Bettys at Morotia."

Corp. Henry T. Stephenson, 130 Maple, River Rouge: "Saidor and Aitape were picnics compared to the Buna campaign.

We were able to use an ambulance for the first time at Aitape. We thought the 32nd was going home after Aitape. But the Philippines were ahead.

"Leyte was the toughest of anything. Then came Luzon—rougher and tougher yet. Nothing was harder than the Villa Verde. The Japs had plenty of artillery. They zeroed in. There were no safe holes anywhere."

Sergt. Henry F. Domanowski, 3880 Yemans, Hamtramck: "Coming into Leyte for the landing, our division's convoy was hit by Jap torpedo planes. We watched the Jap torpedoes zoom into the water. A Liberty Ship went down. A Jap torpedo crashed less than 100 yards from our LST."

Corp. Chester Czarnowski, 6462 Craig, Detroit: "The Japs ambushed our ambulances on the Ormoc highway. They sprayed the ambulances, though their sides showed big Red Crosses. We jumped into the ditch. When the infantrymen were hit and dropped their rifles, we picked them up and fought—to save our patients."

« 66 »

Battle Casualties Are Always Game

THE YANK BATTLE CASUALTY is a magnificent fellow. Right out of the front lines with his body torn and sore from Jap bullets, hand grenades, mortars or artillery shell fragments—he never whimpers.

He is grateful to be alive!

And the first thing he does, the first conscious moment he has, he writes or has written for him a letter of reassurance to the Only Girl back home. She may be his wife. She may be the mother of a son or a daughter he has never seen. She may be a sweetheart he will marry when he gets "back stateside."

But he writes to her, groggy, half unconscious, sometimes just recalled from the valley of the beyond by medical science.

He writes to her that—his wounds are minor.

He doesn't want the Only Girl to worry!

That's the kind of a gent he is, this Yank battle casualty.

Twenty-one Michigan life-savers sang the praises of the battle casualty—the front-line wounded veteran—with the same haunting, never-to-be-forgotten refrain of a Stephen Foster song.

They, too, have been in the combat zone.

A platoon of the medics were almost surrounded by Japs in Manila as they rushed to the aid of internees retaken from the Japs. The infantry shot them to freedom by killing the Japs in their way. They know war, and the temperament, the character of the Yank battle casualty.

The Michigan medics will tell you.

"The wounded Yank is a great . . . the grandest gent in the world," said Corp. James Vaughan, 1968 Wyoming avenue, Dearborn. "He takes his wounds—and sometimes those wounds are really rough—as a matter of course. He considers himself lucky to be alive—what a guy!"

"Wounded front-line soldiers are a bunch of good Joes," said Elmer A. Parrott, 1192 Seventh street, Muskegon, a ward surgical technician. "They are so appreciative of what we do for them that, my gosh, you just have to break your neck for those guys!"

The civilian internee, rescued by these soldiers, often is "the champion hospital griper of them all," and the so-called "base commandos," the rear echelon soldiers, are the most demanding of the hospital's patients.

So said Sergt. Matthew M. Skerjance, of 3349 Mallory avenue, Flint, a ward surgical technician.

"The battle casualty never hollers for attention," he said. "Whatever you do for him is okay—as long as you help him."

"As soon as those boys can even move a finger," said Pfc. Arthur J. Dickson, 2482 Beals avenue, Detroit, "they want to write a letter to their wife or to their sweetheart. They want their Best Girl to know they are all right."

"I had a battle casualty from Michigan," recalled Corp. John A. Potenza, 72 Temple street, Detroit, a ward technician. "He had a tough time for five days just keeping alive. But he didn't want his wife to know how seriously wounded he was. Said it might scare her."

"What really gets me," said Corp. Edmun E. Cram, of 439 Delaware street, Grand Rapids, "is the way they worry about a wounded pal.

"I had a patient with a stomach wound. His case was serious. Right in the operating room he asked us to 'Look after my pal behind me.' And his pal only had a broken arm!"

When I saw Corp. Harry A. Warner, of 4589 Helen avenue, Dearborn, he had nine letters from home, including a birthday greeting from his folks, his biggest "batch of letters in a long time."

He was a very proud corporal, but over another letter, a letter to his folks by a wounded soldier who had recovered in his ward.

"And what do you think he did! He got home all right, completely recovered. Why he wrote my folks a letter, the grandest letter you ever saw. What a guy!"

A garrison soldier may go to the medics 10 times a day when he has athlete's foot, but let him get wounded in action and he never whimpers, never complains, observed Sergt.-Maj. Kenneth D. Eagle, whose home town is in Flint, his wife lives in Marshall and his folks live in Davison.

"What a Joe the battle casualty is," he said.

"He never whimpers. I know a soldier who had an arm blown off and all he wrote to his wife was, 'Don't worry, honey; I'm coming home to you. Please don't worry.'"

Suicide Planes Attack Medics Too

« 67 »

THE SURGEONS and the doctors, the ambulance drivers and the litter bearers, the operating technicians and the ward technicians of the 41st Field Hospital were on a Liberty Ship going from Biak to Luzon.

Then the Jap suicide bombers attacked!

The medical Liberty Ship was only one in a vast convoy. The medics were sitting on the deck, some sunning themselves, some playing cards, some just talking.

They saw two Navy airships fly overhead. Not much later, they saw six fighters high above them.

"We thought they were ours, of course," said Capt. Donald G. Bills, of 915 Verlinden avenue, Lansing. "Then they peeled off. They picked us out. They picked out ships on both sides of us. They came down in terrible dives. Suddenly, we knew the worst. They were Jap suicide dive bombers.

"We found that out when our ack-ack opened up. It got one near us. But another ship near us was hit hard twice."

The medics did not get panicky. They were veterans of Biak, and of Milne Bay in New Guinea.

"We had a hot time in Biak," said Capt. Bills. "The Jap made it hot. I flew in there with three others and two and a half tons of equipment. We went through Jap bombings. We had to sleep on the ground. We could hear the bombs from the Jap Bettys singing. We hugged the ground in our foxholes —and it was hard work digging foxholes on the coral island of Biak."

So the medics who had been through that knew how to take the worst!

"I was sitting on the deck playing cards when the suicide Jap planes hit the convoy," said Sergt. Duncan MacNicol, of 2437 Antoinette street, Detroit, a ward master. "One of them came down trying to get our ship. It started peeling off. I didn't think it could miss—but it was shot down! We went down in the hole of the ship."

"We sat in that hole for 25 minutes," said Sergt. Howard M. Gowing, 5641 Middlesex avenue, Dearborn. "We just sat there, so far below water level. We could hear our guns. It was something to think about, not knowing what happened.

"After that, when we had air warnings, I hit on the deck. I liked that better not being fenced in. But the Japs didn't come back. They had enough, I guess."

So the 41st got safely to Luzon to do the grand job it has done for the wounded.

It was activated at Camp Ellis, Ill., July 16, 1943, with 16 per cent of its personnel from Michigan. It reached this area in April to support the infantry driving on Baguio.

But the 41st was a veteran outfit by then. It had been at Milne Bay in New Guinea. Then it was transported entirely by air to support the 41st Division at Biak. In Luzon it supported the 43rd Division at Manaoag, and the 37th, the 6th Division, and the 1st Cavalry in the drive on Manila in the early days of the return campaign in the Philippines.

Its personnel rushed with the infantry to Santa Tomas and Bilibid prison camps for Americans—Jap prison camps under the long Japanese occupation.

And in these instances, the hospital personnel worked long hours to save the half-starved internees, so long denied proper attention.

The 41st has been overseas for 16 months, and it has seven months of operation in combat zones.

"I think we have done a good job," said Capt. Leo Kagan, of New York City, the unit's adjutant. "At least the hospital personnel has worked hard. Never complained about long hours. Never worried about the clock.

"But I think that wounded Yanks have always inspired everybody, from the surgeons all the way done the line. The American wounded are the grandest people in the world!

"We are happy — and proud — that we have pulled most of them through!"

« 68 »

Medics Scorn Snipers

THERE WAS BITTER fighting going on in the streets and buildings of Manila when the decision was made to try to get a platoon of the 41st Field Hospital to Bilibid prison. There were many Yank internees there, long the prisoners of war of the Japs. Some of them needed medical attention desperately. The medics are not fighting men. They have no riflemen, mortar sections, or field artillery. Nothing like that. Only the equipment, the personnel to use it, and the will to save lives of a crack hospital.

They went in!

"I was in a two and a half ton truck the first day going into Bilibid," said Sergt. Ralph M. Ware, of 69 Lincoln avenue, Mt. Clemens.

"As we eased in, there was street fighting a half block away. We stopped. It looked as if we had stopped right in the middle of the whole blankety-blank war.

"An infantry officer ran up. 'Hold it, fellows,' he said. 'Snipers up ahead, a lot of them. We'll knock 'em off and get you through.'

"Why, he stood out like a target, just waving his men forward, shouting, 'Move up men, move up. Got to get these medics in. Let's go.'"

The medics watched the infantry. The riflemen, the tommygunners, the grenade throwers moved up in a half crouch, but always forward, slowly forward.

"We heard the Jap snipers open up," he continued. "Then our boys let go. They really knew their stuff. Japs started falling all over the place. Finally, this officer yelled to one of the surgeons:

"'Hey, Doc, go on in, we got those blankety-blanks!'

"And he went in. I never saw so many newly dead Japs in my life sprawled all over the place. These infantry guys sure made a bunch of pals that day in our outfit."

The next day Sergt. William H. Bock, of 4790 State street, Saginaw, was with a truck load of medics of the 41st still bent on joining the first group at Bilibid. The call had gone out. More medics wanted!

The street fighting was still going on in Manila. But the medics never hesitated. They brought needed medical supplies and more medical technicians in.

"The street fighting was all over the place as we crept slowly in toward Bilibid in our truck convoy," said Sergt. Bock.

"But by this time the Japs were out to stop us. I guess they knew what we were up to. They put in an artillery road block on our route. Our artillery and our infantry gnawed away at it.

"So we were stopped by artillery shells for a time. But the convoy finally got in—with most of its tires shot up. But we got the medical supplies in. That was the important thing. We went right through that road block with the help of our boys, finally. A lot of dead Japs, too, lying around."

Some of the ambulance drivers for the 41st had a rugged go of it, too, while they were on detached service with the 43rd Division and the 1st Cavalry. Ambulance drivers like Pfc. Richard P. Roraff, 14818 Rossini avenue, Detroit.

"I was running an ambulance from a clearing station to an

air strip to an evacuation hospital, during that fighting at Manaoag," recalled Roraff.

"I was moving along with four patients. The Filipino guerillas stopped me. One of them said, 'Snipers up ahead, Joe. Wait.'

"So I waited 20 minutes on the road, under a palm tree. I heard a lot of shooting. Finally the Filipino officer came back, 'All right now, Joe,' he said. 'Get the wounded in. We got Japs —plenty of Japs—with our American stuff.'

"Away I went.

"Later, I had to make a 54-mile haul down from the mountains in that operation, with my ambulance full of patients. Had to go carefully. Sometimes the Jap patrols were out looking for our ambulances.

"I would drive five or ten miles an hour. Sometimes I went so slow the ambulance just dragged along. But the patients never whimpered—and I was always glad to get them in!"

« 69 »

Doctors and Cooks Combine to Save Lives

A TOPNOTCH FIELD hospital like the 41st is necessarily operated by a group of specialists.

It is mechanized. It is portable. It can haul down its tents and ride away to the combat zones in a few hours. It brings the finest surgeons, the best doctors, and expert medical technicians right up to where the wounded Yank and the sick American soldier need them most.

Never farther back than an ambulance ride. Not too close to the front for the comfort and recovery of the wounded. But close enough.

Every man in its personnel is a specialist who knows his

stuff and watches his own batting average like an American League ball player. For war is the Big League of the medics anywhere.

For example, Sergt. Harold F. Laycock, of Sturgis, Mich., is a pharmacist. One of his major responsibilities is to see that the vital penicillin is always on hand. It saves so many lives in so many ways.

"I guess I must have handled several hundred thousand bottles of penicillin," Sergt. Laycock said. "I get 25,000 vials of it at a time. There was a time, as at Biak, when we had a hard time getting everything. Now we have an abundance of all supplies. Once in a while we are held up a few hours on something. But not longer. The Army planners really roll in what we need. And that saves a lot of lives."

I talked to a couple of first cooks. They are as proud of the job they do as the surgeons. Perhaps my old friend, Dr. Nate Schlafer of Detroit, once chief surgeon at Receiving Hospital, will agree with them.

They like to keep the patients well fed. They claim the best mess in the Southwest Pacific. I have to agree with them. The food was so good and the water so cold at their meals, I hated to leave.

"We have served as many as 980 a day," said Sergt. Joseph Ozella, 453 Canton street, Detroit. "If the meals aren't good I hope those wounded boys knock my skull in.

"We have meat twice a day, pork chops and beef. Today we had big American hamburgers. Yesterday, meat loaf. Sometimes ice cream. And cold cokes for the patients."

"I like the hefty appetites the patients have," said Sergt. Gerald E. Cook, 12830 Glenfield street, Detroit, the other first cook. "They come to us after eating K-rations and Ten-in-Ones. Boy, what appetites. They eat like horses. It is fun cooking for those guys. All they do is praise the food—and eat."

Sergt. Nelson E. Short, 1114 Underwood avenue, Grand Rapids, was listening.

"I had a good meal," he said, "after the Japs tried to wipe out our convoy with their suicide bombers. I'd heard of that stuff. I didn't think they really would do it. But I saw it. Nothing like a good meal after that. But six Jap pilots never ate again. "

The women do most of the work in the Philippines. The other day I saw 50 of them digging ditches to keep the rain water out of their front yards—while the Filipino men took siestas in their nipa huts.

But a crew of 25 Filipinos work hard for the 41st Field, digging ditches to keep the rainy season's torrents out of the wards. They also act as carriers of supplies and as manual laborers for the hospital's camp.

"You have to know how to talk to them," said Pfc. Leonard Mancuso, of 3560 Gladwin avenue, Detroit. "You can't bawl them out. You can't scold them. You can't drive them. I just take them through the wards and give them a look at our boys. They sure work like blazes after that!"

"You can say that in high," said Pfc. Harold F. King, of Greenville. "Whenever I get tired in my ward I just think of those wounded kids lying there. They are so appreciative of what you do for them."

"I found out all about the war from those uncomplaining wounded Joes," said Pfc. Raymond J. Brzezniak, of Manistee. "They are a nice bunch of boys. The wounded in my ward have always been easy to take care of."

I enjoyed talking to Pfc. John F. Stoneham, of Hart. It was a nostalgic enjoyment. He had the word "Michigan" painted across his fatigue cap.

Stoneham was a chum of Milton Pugsley, of Hart, the son of Judge Earl C. Pugsley, my old friend, whom I admired so much as the trial judge in all the graft conspiracy cases growing out of the Ferguson-O'Hara grand jury investigation in Detroit a few years ago.

"Milt is an ensign now," he said. "A Navy guy. Sure like to see him for a few minutes. Like to tell him how our wounded can take it."

« 70 »

It's Painful to Say Goodbye

SOMETIMES, it seems, the most painful word in our language is goodbye. So many millions of our boys have said goodbye to the home folks. In the combat zone, somebody is always taking off and leaving old friends behind.

After the nine weeks with the fighting 32nd Division, it was hard to say goodbye. For the Red Arrow boys are some of the grandest fellows in the world.

I saw them in action in one of their toughest operations in three years of fighting, the rough scrap on the Villa Verde Trail. It was a slugging match in the mountains at close-up with the Japs. The Red Arrow boys did so many incredible things in the Caraballo Mountains. Even the routine on the Villa Verde was amazing.

I lived and slept, groused and exulted with these veterans. I sweated out the Jap snipers with them on the Villa Verde, and later I swam in the surf of the Pacific with resting veterans. Heard their laughter. Felt their gayety. Saw them discard the grimness of war at play like you would change your clothes back home.

And so as you go along at war, you make friends, quickly because the dreadful continuity of war brings a fast mutuality of interest. I made a lot of friends.

But a war correspondent is a lonesome guy. Just when he

is comfortable, just when he is surrounded by GI's and officers whom he likes, he must take off. It's one of those things. The war in the Pacific is so vast, great distances have been reduced to whistle stops on the airship routes, and there are so many combat zones calling. They always haunt you.

It was toughest of all saying goodbye to Maj. Gen. W. H. Gill, the commander of the Red Arrow. On the surface he seems like the hard-boiled leader of a hard-boiled division. But he is a very human guy with a vast understanding of people, their dreams, their ambitions, their illusions. There really wasn't very much to say.

At the last moment, he gave me a copy of the Red Arrow's historical pamphlet, "13,000 Hours of Combat." I had wanted one. But only a few copies were printed. They were scheduled to go to the relatives of the dead and to the wounded who had been evacuated to the states.

"You might look on page three," Gen. Gill said in his quiet voice. "I took the liberty of writing something for you."

Well, hell, I read it and re-read it. I knew he meant every word of it. There is no fake in Gen. Gill. He wrote things that put a quick catch in your throat. So I sent the pamphlet home to my two boys. It was like that.

The last night I was with the Red Arrow it rained, as only it can rain in the Orient. The USO was putting on Oklahoma up ahead. I had seen it twice, but I started out in my battered jeep, the one Lt. Verne G. Jubenville, of 5346 Burns avenue, Detroit, named The Amphibious Mouse Trap.

So I ran a hitch-hiker's special for the GI's for the 20-mile trip to see Oklahoma. It was a lot of fun. We were all soaked to the skin. But they wanted to see Oklahoma in the rain and they saw it.

I stopped at the Dew Drop Inn in a little town to get in out of the rain. There I met Sergt. Fred L. Gilliland, Jr., of 2942 Cass avenue, Detroit.

He had been fighting with the 3rd Battalion of the 128th Infantry, with a rifle squad, on the Villa Verde. Fred is a first class fighting man and a pretty swell gent. As he took off in the rain, finally, he shouted through the downpour, "See you in Detroit—keep your head down!"

A little later I picked up Pfc. Karl R. Hauter, 18269 Robson avenue, Detroit, a machine gunner who had fought at Balete Pass with the 33rd Infantry Division. The rain was streaming down his face as he got in the jeep, but it couldn't hide the big grin as we talked about things back home.

So the next day, when I was scheduled to take off, the division did another nice thing. The Amphibious Mouse Trap had to be brought back to the Red Arrow. So, Corp. Thaddeus Kziazek (and you guessed it, of 4628 Plumer avenue, Detroit), a cavalry recon veteran of 39 months overseas, was assigned to make the 8-hour trip.

No ride could be dull with Teddy. He was out in the Jap lines with the recon only recently. Two riflemen were taken sick. Teddy was given the job to get them into our lines. He got them in. But it took four days. Twice they were ambushed by the Japs. But they took to "the bush," and hiked their way through the mountains.

Some of the Filipino roads were tough. We hit an overgrown boulder and knocked a hole in the oil pan. So we dropped into the 289th Ordnance Company.

The Detroit boys overseas always take care of their own. Sergt. Bruce H. Van Tifflin, 12820 Appoline avenue, Detroit, an ordance mechanic, worked two hours under the jeep getting it ready to run again.

Up came two other Detroiters—Sergt. Antonio J. Vogliano, 244 East Grande avenue, Highland Park, and Pfc. George Aprahamian, 16532 Parkside avenue, both mechanics—to give Sergt. Van Tifflin some good natured advice.

That night Teddy and I went to the Club Ciro, where they

have a hot dance band and serve a drink called Gimlet at Two Dollars a throw just to keep in practice with hitting the liberators of the Philippines with a peso-edged hatchet.

We met up with six rough-and-tumble guys from the 11th Airborne, in Manila on a three-day pass after making a jump at Apari. Rugged guys, the airborne. They had the orchestra working overtime on their favorite song.

It was, "Don't Fence Me in."

« 71 »

Yamashita

With the 32d Infantry Division in Northern Luzon, Sept. 2
AT 0800 THIS MORNING, after 41 months of fighting, veteran infantrymen of the 32d (Red Arrow) Division got their first glimpse of the man who had been their toughest adversary, Lieutenant General Tomoyuki Yamashita, Supreme Japanese commander in the Philippines.

At exactly 0800 General Yamashita, his onetime 200 pound bulk shrunken to 165 pounds, delivered himself smiling to a 24-man honor guard from I Company on the 32d's 128th Infantry Regiment at an outpost three kilometers from Kiangan.

Ten thirty found Yamashita sitting in a battered schoolhouse at Kiangan while the representatives of his Emperor aboard the Battleship Missouri in Tokyo Bay, were signing the terms of "unconditional surrender." It was the "Tiger of Malaya" himself who, three and a half years ago at the fall of Singapore, first used the term, "unconditional surrender," in the Pacific War. The man to whom he dictated those terms, General Perceval, was standing at General MacArthur's elbow on the Missouri.

The man who had directed stubborn Japanese mountain

defenses on Leyte and Luzon was smiling and pleasant as he turned himself and his staff over to the 32d honor guard. The General and his 11 companions were standing on a hilltop at a previously arranged rendezvous when Lieutenant Russell Bauman, of Glen Beulah, Wisc., and his veteran riflemen approached.

Yamashita and his staff saluted. Lt. Bauman returned the salute and said, "I have the honor to inform you that I have been charged with seeing you and your party through our lines without hindrance, delay or molestation."

Yamashita, who speaks no English, said through an interpreter, "I want to tell you how much I appreciate the courtesy and good treatment you have shown us." He repeated this phrase often throughout the entire morning.

Attired in a clean but worn uniform and wearing his sword and ribbons, the Japanese General appeared to be in good health in spite of his loss of weight. He puffed only slightly at the exertion of a three kilometer walk to the I Company Command Post in the schoolhouse at Kiangan. As he mopped his brow with an immaculate handkerchief, he revealed a shaven head. The route led over a rough mountain trail. All the officers wore their swords and decorations pinned on open-necked silk shirts.

At I Company CP Yamashita was met by Colonel Ernest A. Barlow, of Salt Lake City, Utah, Chief of Staff of the 32d Division, and Lieutenant Colonel Alex Robinet, of Fort Thomas, Kentucky, Commander of the 128th Infantry.

The party was delayed for two hours at Kiangan while vehicles ploughed through washed-out roads to reach the group. It was during this time that the surrender pact was signed at Tokyo. Yamashita occupied himself eating Army K-rations with obvious enjoyment and signing short-snorter bills for GIs.

Lieutenant General Muto, the "Tiger's" Chief of Staff, asked Colonel Barlow the significance of the Red Arrow insignia on his shoulder. Colonel Barlow replied that it was the insignia of the 32d Division and that it symbolized the 32d's breaching of the Hindenburg Line in World War I.

General Muto replied, "Yes, and the Yamashita Line in World War II."

Yamashita and his party were driven to the First Battalion Command Post of the 128th for lunch and hence to the airstrip at Bagabag, where a C-47 transport was waiting to take the General and his staff to Baguio where formal surrender terms will be signed tomorrow at Camp John Hay.

When the honor guard first met the Jap General this morning, a Major Toguchi, who acted as courier for Yamashita, requested that a sedan chair be provided for the supreme commander. The request was refused by Captain Ray A. Glisson, of Washington, D.C., I Company Commander, who handled the arrangements for the 32d Division.

Major Toguchi asked red-headed, blue-eyed Captain Glisson whether he was Irish. "Yeah," replied Glisson, "are you?"

For the GIs of the 32d this was a great day. At long last the war had really ended for Red Arrow men as for everyone else. This Division fought its way from Buna in New Guinea to Luzon in the Philippines, amassing 654 days combat in World War II. These infantrymen had faced and defeated Yamashita first in Leyte's Ormoc Corridor and then again in 119 days of bitter fighting on Northern Luzon's Villa Verde Trail.

The 32d killed more than 15,000 of Yamashita's troops in the Philippines fighting. They completely shattered the "Tiger's" Imperial First Division on Leyte. It was the 32d which had tracked the "scourge of the Philippines" to his end.

Yamashita is surrendering an estimated 32,000 troops on Luzon. Ten thousand of these require medical care. The Japanese are being provided with equipment and medicines to set up their own hospital units under U. S. Army supervision.